Praise for *Watch and Wonder*

"As Thoreau once said, 'Think of our life in nature,—daily to be shown matter, to come in contact with it.' The bird, flitting into our overstimulated consciousness, is the perfect example; as this fine book makes clear, the chance to pay attention is a great gift."

—**Bill McKibben**, author, environmental activist, and Schumann Distinguished Scholar, Middlebury College

"Sutterfield not only educates about birds; he shows how to think *with* birds. Ancient monks, distinguished theologians, and nature philosophers ride along with him on his feathered explorations into nature's rhythms and rituals."

—**Trish O'Kane**, author of *Birding to Change the World*

"I feel like I have glimpsed something of God in the azure flash of a tiny indigo bunting and the sublime grandeur of a bald eagle's gaze. In this wise and inviting book, Sutterfield helps us understand the wondrous intersection of Creator and creation in these beings who defy gravity. Read this book to learn how to listen and look for feathered companions who teach us to lift up our hearts."

—**James K. A. Smith**, Calvin University, author of *How to Inhabit Time* and *Make Your Home in This Luminous Dark*

"I met Ragan Sutterfield early in my journey into wild church. He is a fellow edgewalker and pioneer in integrating the holy mystery of the natural world with the Christian faith. In this intimate book, *Watch and Wonder*, Ragan shares his experiences of the Holy through his relationship with a series of common birds, stretching the understanding of beloved community beyond those of our own church or our own species. These stories offer a gift of sacramental sight through the lives of birds as apostles of mystery while staying rooted in the sacraments of the church. Nature and Spirit are, in fact, not separate."

—**Victoria Loorz**, author of *Church of the Wild* and *Field Guide to Church of the Wild* and host of *The Holy Wild* podcast

"As a birder, I loved *Watch and Wonder*. As a pastor, I found myself saying amen on every page. Through birding and its myriad of challenges and delights, Ragan Sutterfield guides us in patient attention and persistent hope, helping us listen to 'a quiet world ready to speak' and, in so doing, open ourselves anew to the voice of God."

—**Courtney Ellis**, author of *Looking Up: A Birder's Guide to Hope Through Grief*

"For anyone who has been curious about birdwatching, Ragan Sutterfield's lyrical love letter to this pastime is a wonderful place to start. Beyond the inherent joy of seeing a flash of brilliant color at the birdfeeder or hearing the mournful hoot of an owl on a forest walk, the birds provide us with a way of paying attention to, and thus loving, the created world. May *Watch and Wonder* restore our amazement at the variety, beauty, and interdependence of creation—and our commitment to care for it as our home."

—**Katelyn Beaty**, author, editor, and lifelong birdwatcher

"This is an extraordinary book. In *Watch and Wonder*, Sutterfield invites contemplation of God's wild, weird, and wounded world through the spiritual practice of birding. This is not a birdwatching book. It is an invitation to active and patient engagement with creatures of extravagant color and character in their individuality, as revelatory of the God who made them and us. Paying attention, lingering in astonishment to the point of love and solidarity with birds and their places in the world is the invitation the book offers. I especially loved that Sutterfield's Christian imagination, formed and informed by liturgy, theological study, and the stories of scripture, frames a seeing of both the glory and brokenness of the world through the lens of birding. It is as though birding also participates in the history of redemption."

—**Rev. Richard R. Topping**, PhD, president and vice chancellor of Vancouver School of Theology

WATCH AND WONDER

RAGAN SUTTERFIELD

WATCH AND WONDER

BIRDING AS A SPIRITUAL PRACTICE

Broadleaf Books
Minneapolis

WATCH AND WONDER
Birding as a Spiritual Practice

30 29 28 27 26 2 3 4 5 6 7 8 9

Library of Congress Control Number: 2025033596 (print)

Cover image: © 2025 Getty Images/Moments Collection; Old chromolithograph illustration of Songbirds by mikroman6
Cover design: Broadleaf Books/Alisha Lofgren

Print ISBN: 979-8-8898-3261-4
eBook ISBN: 979-8-8898-3262-1

For Bill Shepherd, and the Arkansas birding community,
for welcoming me into this common wonder

CONTENTS

PREFACE

We stood on a platform, overlooking a small lake, our scopes scanning the water. It was late fall, and the winter birds were beginning to arrive—raptors and ducks, sparrows and gulls. This was one of the best places to see them all: Holla Bend National Wildlife Refuge. The refuge had been a frequent haunt of my days as a young birder, beginning on Audubon Society field trips and then continuing in high school and college. For two years, my summer job was studying Kentucky Warblers in the river-bottom lands of Holla Bend. Now I was here, middle-aged, my life very different from what I imagined as a teenaged birder who dreamed of being an ornithologist or birding tour guide.

On the platform with me was Evan. Both of us are Episcopal priests, and we were theoretically on a clergy retreat. The schedule made the mistake of giving us a large chunk of free time, however, and Evan and I had taken advantage, driving from the retreat center to the nearby wildlife refuge. By this point in the day, we'd overshot the break by several hours and were now well into the afternoon presentations. Neither of us were too worried about having played hooky. After all, as Evan explained to the other priests at the retreat over our evening game of poker, birding is a spiritual practice.

But how? I've been thinking about that question ever since I began to pursue the life of prayer that led me toward priesthood. Why was it that watching birds seemed to be as formative for the deepest parts of my life as more traditional spiritual practices? In what ways did birding echo those more conventional habits of the soul?

Spiritual practices, at their best, are activities that help us become the kinds of people the world needs now. In religious traditions they are usually things like prayer and fasting and meditation. In recent years, people outside of traditional religious circles have recognized the power of such practices for their own lives of fullness. Whether religious or not, the things to which we give our attention and the activities we do with intention can have profound impacts on who we are. Birding is no different.

In reflecting on my own life as a birder, from my earliest days as an obsessed teenager to my current life as an amateur, I found a number of ways that birding can be a spiritual practice. This book is an attempt to explore twelve of them.

As a Christian priest I bring my reading, tradition, and experiences as a lens through which I understand these practices, but I hope that people of other faiths or no faith at all will find my reflections useful. At its heart this is a book born of my love for birds and the people who watch and wonder at their lives.

One of the formative realities of birding is the way it helps us inhabit time. Paying attention to birds puts us into contact with the seasons in a world where so much of our life is disconnected from natural rhythms. For this reason, it felt right to center the journey of this book around a birder's year, the calendar serving as a place to bring my experiences, both past and present, into conversation.

Whether you are a serious birder that drops everything to chase a rarity or a backyard birder who enjoys the common species of your neighborhood, I hope that *Watch and Wonder* will deepen your love for winged and wild creatures and draw you into a deeper care for their plight. There is beauty and hope and healing if we slow down and pay attention.

Little Rock, Arkansas
Feast of Julian of Norwich, 2025

1

JANUARY

Icons

I SIT AT a desk that I bought at a place that sells the discarded furniture of offices. It is an antique of sorts, made of solid wood, scratched and pocked here and there, with rings from coffee cups at a comfortable arm's reach. Outside I hear a Blue Jay—loud, smart, and beautiful, they seem forever young, the bold teenagers of the bird world. Quieter, a White-throated Sparrow sings its subtle *seeee*, a note signaling *I am here, all is well.* Most of the year I could see these birds from the window before me. But it is winter, and I've covered the drafty single pane of glass with plastic, in an attempt to keep my writing shed warm. The small space heater hums along as high as I can turn it without tripping the breaker.

On the wall below the window hangs a collection of icons and a crucifix. The icons are mounted on wood, mostly cheap laminates printed and glued on. But one, an image of the Madonna and Child, was hand painted with halos of gold paint, a gift from a friend who made a trip to Eastern Europe many years ago.

The religious tradition in which I grew up had no place for icons. When I was in church as a child, we were more likely to see videos projected on screens than these strange, holy images mounted on wood or printed on cards and laminated in plastic. It wasn't until college that I really even knew icons existed. I'd go to a Catholic bookstore not far from campus and look around, curious at the alien and yet familiar forms of worship—the same God, the same basic beliefs, but so different in culture. I bought a prayer card there with an icon of "Christ the Teacher" on one side and a prayer of St. Ephrem on the other. It was my first icon, and I still have it, here, propped alongside the others.

Icons strike me with an alluring strangeness. The figures are flat, and realism is not the goal, clearly. Yet they somehow invite me into a reality—something I can't quite name or subject to analysis. To pray with an icon, I am told, is to look at an image that invites the eye beyond it, out and into the very heart of God.

The Catholic priest and writer Henri Nouwen notes that "icons are not easy to 'see.' . . . They do not reveal themselves to us at first sight. It is only gradually, after patient, prayerful presence that they start to speak." Despite the icons before me, I'm not sure that I have yet really "seen" them in the sense of which Nouwen speaks. But his language reminds me of birds, who are also not always easy to see, especially at first sight. I have caught a glimpse of birds and, like icons, they have opened me to a wider wonder.

When I was around twelve years old, my younger brother went with some friends to a workshop at a local state park. He returned with a bird feeder, and my parents set it up on our back deck, just outside our living room windows. We lived, at the time, in a suburban neighborhood on the west side of Little Rock, Arkansas. Whether for aesthetics or because the developers couldn't make the subdivision grid match the hilly landscape, our house backed up to a tract of uncut forest, maybe ten acres or so, that, though surrounded by housing developments, remains intact to this day. The woods, a mix of oaks, hickories, and pines with a couple of creeks running through them, made our feeder attractive to a better-than-average variety of birds. Far more species than I had imagined existing were suddenly at my window.

We had a set of encyclopedias in the living room, a set of hand-me-down World Books, hardbound in off-white and with green decorations. In the "B" volume there was an article about birds, including a full-spread color plate with common backyard species. There was a picture of a Tufted Titmouse, resembling a small gray cardinal, its crest raised in alert, its pink sides a soft touch of subtle elegance. Then there were the chickadees—the Black-capped species was pictured in the encyclopedia. I had yet to learn that in Arkansas we have only Carolina Chickadees, with their nearly identical Black-capped cousins ranging farther north and west. Then there were the Northern Cardinals, the birds my grandfather, an avid feeder of birds himself, called "Red Birds." Blue Jays and American Crows were included, as were White-breasted Nuthatches and Dark-eyed Juncos, American Robins, and Brown Thrashers.

It was a fair if limited start, twenty species or so of the ten thousand bird species in the world, the more than three hundred possible to see in Arkansas. It didn't take long for me to exhaust the guidance of the World Book, as many birds that simply weren't on the plates arrived at the feeders.

Though I didn't quite know it at the time, I was taking on a new identity, entering a tribe of people who give their time and money and attention to the feathered world. I was becoming a birder. In those days birders were a small circle of enthusiasts, but like a rapidly growing religion, it has spread, one encounter of wonder at a time. Decades later, when the COVID-19 pandemic slowed the world down and the noise of machines was temporarily quieted, many more people began to pay attention to the birds that share their world. Since then birding has exploded, with participant estimates going as high as a third of the US adult population. Whether backyard observers or serious "chasers" of rarities, most of us began as I did, with an encounter that drove us to look for more.

Birders sometimes talk about their "spark bird": the individual bird, or species, that suddenly created a portal into an entire new world. That encounter becomes a blaze that takes a person from being a normal human being—one who sees birds all the time but doesn't pay much attention to them—to the kind of person who spends thousands of dollars and hour upon hour looking for birds. If I had to name one, my spark bird would be the Pine Warbler—a small songbird with an olive yellow back, bright yellow chest, white wing bars, and a white ring framing a curious dark eye. A common, year-around resident in Arkansas, this is a bird that, appropriate to its name, is found nearly anywhere there is a decent stand of pine trees.

When a Pine Warbler first showed up at my feeder, the only bird that matched its yellow in the encyclopedia was a Goldfinch. I knew, somehow, that this was a different kind of bird—the beak was too thin to be a finch, and it lacked the black on the forehead and wings. I felt a stirring to know its name.

My dad had a camera, but there was no telephoto lens in his camera bag. So, to get a good picture of a bird, I had to get close. I set the camera on a tripod by the bird feeder, draped a sheet over myself, and waited patiently for a bird to land. Sometimes I'd set a scene, placing daffodils on the feeder, hoping for a Pine Warbler to come—the bright yellow of the flower and the bird complementing one another. A warbler would come and, with a camera click, the bird's wings would lift, the light of the moment captured in gelatin and silver. I had the bird recorded, but I still didn't know its name.

The early Christian centuries were full of conflict, the basic beliefs of the new religion settling toward coherence. What began as a Jewish movement morphed in its pagan context, and as with any transmission of ideas to a new setting, the question came: What is essential and what is merely cultural?

Judaism, like Islam after it, had a strict prohibition against creating images of the divine. This was a foundational precept from the very beginning of the faith and for good reason. Israel defined the nature of their God as uncontainable, beyond capture or manipulation. While other faiths had made the divine presence accessible through statues or images, Judaism articulated a vision of God as being so beyond the creatures of this world that no form could be given to God's being. God made all things and sustained all things. How could one represent the fullness of such a being without in some way violating it? To make no graven image of God was even codified in the Ten Commandments, the greatest statement of Jewish law.

Christians followed Judaism, accepting the Ten Commandments as authoritative but with a radical twist. This God who had made all things and sustained all things had, in some impossible to fully explain way, entered the human frame. Jesus, the anointed Christ, was not simply the long-awaited Messiah; he was God.

If God was a human, and humans can be pictured in images, then wouldn't it follow that Jesus, who was God, could be pictured without falling into idolatry? This was a question that raged across the early Christian world. By the eighth century came the first of what would be a series of iconoclastic movements throughout Christian history: the emperor of Constantinople ordered that icons be destroyed and statues smashed.

In the Eastern Church, a tradition now known as the center of iconography, the image-destroying side of the debate was eventually overcome by two theologians. John of Damascus, who lived outside the reach of the Christian emperor in an area under Muslim rule, argued that: "In former times, God, without body or form, could in no way be represented. But today, since God has appeared in the flesh and lived among men, I can represent what is visible in God." About a century later, another theologian, Theodore of Studios, who was banished from Constantinople for championing icons, followed John's line of argument to say that "Man has no characteristic more fundamental than this, he can be represented in an image." For him, to deny that Christ could be pictured was to deny the humanity of Christ. His argument eventually won, and though the forces of iconoclasm have risen from time to time, from the Puritans on, the ability to picture the divine has dominated Christian practice. Go to any church with stained-glass windows picturing Jesus, and this will be clear.

In Jesus, we found a God that we can see.

In my young hunger to know the birds that came to my feeder, I met a woman who lived up the street from us, a retiree with a backyard full of birdfeeders and binoculars by the window. She was a "backyard birder," dedicated to caring for and watching the birds beyond her window. I began to visit her regularly, learning from her the names of all those species that were not included in volume B of the encyclopedia. She showed me her *Peterson Field Guide to Birds of Eastern North America*. It had plates with illustrations of almost every recorded bird in the eastern half of North America, with a companion guide to the Western species. In North America the Great Plains had created a rift, resulting in a very different group of species arising on either side. More than by the Mississippi River, the East and West are ecologically divided by the wide-open prairies of the plains.

I used what savings I had to buy my own copy of the Peterson guide, a hardbound edition with a Rose-breasted Grosbeak on the cover. I created little tabs for all the major bird families: ducks, raptors, woodpeckers, warblers, and so on. I had read in a book about birdwatching that such tabs could help me easily find my way through the book. The guide gave me access to a world I never even knew existed—a range of abundant beauty and variety.

Peterson's book, largely credited as the first modern field guide, is illustrated. Like Audubon's *Birds of America* before it, Peterson painted each species. The paintings were organized on plates, grouping similar birds by taxonomy and visual resemblance for easy comparison. When I went to the bookstore to buy the guide, Peterson's stood alongside other field guide offerings, including the *Audubon Society Field Guide to North American Birds*. Originally released in 1977, the Audubon guide was the first to include photographs rather than illustrations.

Though the photographs were excellent, with clear images of each species, I chose the Peterson's illustrated guide. In reading various birding magazines and books, I had been told that an illustrated guide was a better choice as a primary field book, while a photographic guide was a helpful supplement.

It's an odd suggestion, on the face of things. Why would a painting of a bird help you identify it better than a photograph would? Wouldn't a photo be superior to a painting—the real thing better than a human interpretation of it? In a way, the answer goes back to one of the most ancient riddles of philosophy—the question of the one and the many. Is the world made up of many unique, individual things? Or is the world, instead, a unity in which those many things participate? Plato offered an answer through his Theory of Forms. To do injustice to a difficult and complex idea, we could say that the Theory of Forms states that the true essence of things resides in a realm of eidos, or ideas. For instance, there is an ideal form of chair from which the chair I'm sitting in gains its nature. Chairs come in many shapes and sizes, but each has its grounding in this "form of a chair," which exists in the realm of ideas. To look at any individual chair only shows you one unique instance of this essence of chair. It is an old idea, but one to which philosophers have continued to return, because it names a deep truth about the world. In the many resides a deep oneness.

In the case of birds, a painter can look at hundreds of specimens of birds, both in museums and in the field, and illustrate the species in a way that is closer to its ideal, blending the individuals into one "form" of the bird. A photograph, on the other hand, is only a picture of a single bird. The authors of photographic guides try to find birds that are representative, of course; but since every individual has slight variations, that is hard to do consistently. It works far better for Roger Tory Peterson or David Sibley—two of the major bird-guide illustrators of the last century—to look at lots of birds and create an image of the ideal. By looking at the bird before us and then comparing it to the illustration, we are able to see how this individual bird exists within the larger type.

Like an icon, the field guide invites us to look beyond its pages and out to the real world.

The philosopher Jean-Luc Marion offers a helpful distinction between the kinds of images that we'd call an idol and those we'd call an icon. An idol, says Marion, is made when we have an experience of the divine and seek to trap that moment in an object. In a way, it is like a photograph of a bird. An icon, though, does not capture or trap or tame the holy. It gestures toward the divine beyond the image.

Last fall a friend of mine found a Gray-cheeked Thrush, a species not usually seen in Arkansas outside of spring migration. As with a variety of species, this thrush migrates exclusively through the East in the fall. In fact, the bird had never been recorded in our county outside of the spring. I went to the park and found the bird, brown against the ground, hopping from the leaves to a fallen log. I took pictures as it posed, documenting the sides and face, capturing the details that would confirm this bird as the rare species it was for this time of year. It was a moment captured in a digital image by my Nikon. And yet, as the image confirmed the species, it also reflected the individual variations of this particular bird. The spots on its breast were not the exact same as those on the image in the book, the gray on its cheeks was less extensive.

Like a photograph, an idol can fail to capture the fullness of a moment. It is illusory in its concreteness. The encounter is frozen and static, trapped by the light coming into the lens rather than the vision opened by the painted image.

An icon, in Marion's articulation, opens vision rather than closes it. Our eye looks at the image and is invited beyond it. Like a bird illustration, an icon is a representation that draws us toward the field where we can encounter each particular aspect of a bird. Looking at an icon, we are drawn beyond the image. Can birding be like praying with an icon? Could gazing at birds be an opening to a reality beyond the merely visible?

I began to move beyond the backyard by attending the field trips of the Audubon Society of Central Arkansas. A preteen among a group of mostly middle-aged professionals, I was mentored into the culture of birding and the hows of identification. I was introduced to methods of drawing birds out from their hiding places using calls like pishing, a call made by pursing the lips, placing the tongue behind the front teeth, and making a *pish*, *pish*, *pish* sound, or producing a sharp *chip* sound by giving a loud, smacking kiss against the back of your hand. These sounds resemble bird alarm calls, and like nosy neighbors wondering why the police are at the house down the street, the local birds can't resist coming to see what the commotion is about.

Attending Audubon Society field trips was also an entry into an adult world well beyond my parents and their friends. Mel was a writer for magazines like *National Geographic* who yelled excited expletives when a good bird appeared. John worked as an environmental lawyer and later paid my way to join the Audubon Society in a visit to Big Bend National Park. Barry, an environmental and civil rights activist often gave me rides to birding events and exposed me to political ideas far beyond my family's. Lyndal was a professor who chaired the committee that evaluates extraordinary bird records in the state. Through all these people and many more, I was brought into a community of people for whom birding, though not their career, was a light by which they saw the world.

Key among those birders was Bill Shepherd, who must have been in his fifties at the time I met him. He'd been a birder since his teens, and though he'd spent time studying classical literature and botany out of state, he'd returned and birded central Arkansas for more years than anyone. He knew Greek and Latin and could easily rattle off the scientific names of plants and birds. His day job did focus on wild things—plants mostly, but also birds—in his work for the Arkansas Natural Heritage Commission.

The biggest field trip of the year at that time was the annual January visit to Holla Bend National Wildlife Refuge, a river-bottom preserve of little bluestem fields, cedar-lined levees, and lowland hardwood forests. It was a birdy place, full of diverse habitats and species. In the winter it was host to ducks and geese in the tens of thousands, as well as more Western species like Harris Sparrows. It was also a place where Bald Eagles could be seen by the dozens.

The eagles, massive and majestic, made the field trip a special draw even for the most casual birders. For this field trip, the Audubon Society rented a charter bus from Little Rock to the gravel roads of the refuge. Who wouldn't want to see such a wonderful bird, especially from the comfort of a charter bus window?

But having jumped headfirst into the world of birding, I was already sure that I wanted to be with the people who would leave the sightseeing tour behind. We would leave the eagles behind, too, to search the high grass for an elusive Leconte's Sparrow, or venture into the cold and cloudy weather to look among the cedar trees for a roosting Long-eared Owl. When the field trip met at a commuter lot in the early morning, my parents passed me on to a car that included Bill and two other birders, all of us ready to search for the unexpected.

The day delivered. I can't remember the exact list of the birds we found. I know we saw eagles and sparrows, that we walked through the woods and ate brown-bag lunches, leaning against the back of a car, our binoculars always hanging around our necks in case something flew by. After hours passed—every road of the refuge had been driven and most of the trails walked—we decided to call it a day and head home.

We drove out of the refuge and followed the road along the levee that protected fields and houses on the other side from the waters of the Arkansas River. As we drove, we passed through good habitat—open fields with hawks hunting from the edges, along with woodlands interspersed here and there. After a day of looking, we were still on high alert for anything that flew by. Around a bend, Bill shouted, "I think that was a Scissor-tailed Flycatcher!" Rose-flanked and soft gray above, with long tail feathers that open like scissors, these flycatchers are a regular feature in the Arkansas summer landscape. But by fall they've left for a winter in Costa Rica. In January, this would be one very lost bird.

Brantley, who was driving the car, pulled to the shoulder. We poured from it like binocular-clad circus clowns, turning our eyes to the trees around us. I spotted the bird Bill had seen, high up in the bare branches of a cottonwood. I locked my eyes on the bird as I brought my binoculars to my eyes—an old pair of Zeiss Porro prisms that I'd picked up at a pawn shop. Those binoculars, antique by today's standards, were still crisp in their rendering of the bird above.

It was no Scissor-tailed Flycatcher. It had a black cap, and the tail was longer, hanging more like a streamer than the stiff blades of scissors. Even though I had never seen the bird before, I knew it from the field guides I'd studied. "Fork-tailed Flycatcher!" I called out, elated and proud to be the first to identify the bird.

Fork-tailed Flycatchers are Central and South American birds, ranging from the Yucatan of Mexico to the plains of Argentina. Whatever its origin, a Fork-tailed in the Arkansas River Valley was far out of place. This was the first time, in fact, that the species had ever been recorded in the state. All four of us in the car got a chance to watch as the bird flew, searching for flying insects in the cold January air.

The dark soon closed in as the short winter day came to an end. We excitedly drove home toward Little Rock, ready to activate the network of birders through the state rare bird alert, a notification system that operated in those days as a phone call to a regularly updated voicemail recording. Dedicated birders would call to hear what had been seen, especially after weekends when more birders had been in the field.

By the next day, birders from across the state descended on the patch of rural road, photographing the flycatcher. Considered an

American Birding Association area rare bird, it was broadcast to the national rare bird alert. Birders from surrounding states came to see this wandering flycatcher, one that had just happened to be seen by a car full of birders on a January evening.

Though it was not my spark bird, that Fork-tailed Flycatcher has remained a kind of icon for me. It did not invite me to linger on an Arkansas levee but instead drew my eyes beyond it. By seeing this one rare bird, I began to ask: What wonders were passing me by all those years before I learned to pay attention? What wonders are *still* going by that I am unprepared to recognize, too short-sighted or busy to notice? What makes the difference between being able to see such a wonder and letting it pass by?

The world is more amazing than we can grasp. More is happening, stirring, living than any of us can perceive. And so often we miss the extraordinary because our sights are so set on the mundane—fixed on the flat dimensions of the surface. Look at an icon and that's what you get—a poorly rendered, flattened image of a person, sometimes awkwardly positioned. And yet, for an icon, that is precisely the point, because our vision is called to move beyond it. The icon isn't the party but the invitation. But for us to move into the extraordinary, beyond the flat image, we have to change how we see. We have to prepare ourselves for the more when it arrives.

Standing on that roadside, we saw an amazing bird not because it flew past our car but because we had prepared ourselves to recognize it when it came. Bill, with his many decades of birding; me, with all my hours flipping through the field guides. We had cultivated a particular kind of vision that allowed us to see the bird before us. We were ready to see, and so, when the moment came, we did.

Had it been a beetle from Central America rather than a bird, however, I would have missed it. Recognizing this fact calls my mind to another part of seeing: that ultimately there's a kind of grace involved.

The icon offers up the heaven beyond not through the force of practice but rather because we just keep showing up and offering ourselves. Ultimately, it is the world that is beyond us, beautiful and amazing. We have to simply sit before it all with a kind of awe, prepared as best we can to welcome what little light our eyes can perceive. Icons, be they images in paint and wood or creatures of feathers and wings, help us learn to see those small slivers of light and recognize, for a moment, the vastness in which they participate.

To see in this way requires both an openness and recognition. The openness is the ability to let go and imagine new possibilities—it is the work of imagination. Most birders, and indeed most people, miss a good deal because they dismiss the wonderful out of hand: *Oh, it couldn't be this or that*. Skepticism has its place. But if we are unable to entertain the possibilities, then we will never come across a true wonder. We have to start with an openness to what is possible—the reality that the world is always stranger and wilder than we think.

But openness will only get us so far. When the wonderful enters our perception, we have to be ready to recognize it. To be open to the moment of recognition is, in a way, the essence of the contemplative vision. We sit, we walk, we look. We see all kinds of things, but then, in a flash, there is something new, unexpected, a messenger from another world—a Fork-tailed Flycatcher flying across a country road. The philosopher Slavoj Žižek calls such moments an encounter with the "fragile absolute." "What is the Absolute?" asks Žižek. "Something that appears to us in fleeting experiences—say, through the gentle smile of a beautiful woman, or even through the warm caring smile of a person who may otherwise seem ugly and rude. In such miraculous but *extremely fragile* moments, another dimension transpires through our reality. As such, the Absolute is easily corroded; it slips all too easily through our fingers and must be handled as carefully as a butterfly."

The cultivation of such care is what icons help us do. Though it may begin with the extraordinary—the image that finally catches our attention and makes us notice—once our vision has been properly cultivated, we come to see the common things that were always around us with new eyes. A Fork-tailed Flycatcher can be an icon of the rare beauty and drama of the natural world. Then again, so can a White-throated Sparrow—an everyday bird that is beautiful all the same. I've watched them beyond the window, the life and intelligence in their eyes, the subtle yellow of their lores, the gentle broken streaks that run along their backs. Even though I see them by the hundreds each winter, to encounter just one of these is a wonder.

When White-throated Sparrows arrive in my yard each October, as they have done all my life, I now imagine the kind of journey they went through. From a summer in the far north, perhaps the southern borderlands of Canada, they then flew through forests and parks and rested along the brushy edges of drainage ditches in the midst of Midwestern farmlands. They went through all these miles and landscapes to come here, to drink from my bird bath, to hop beneath my elderberry tree singing their song, even in the winter, when it plays no purpose in declaring their territory or attracting a mate. They sing as if to say *I am here*, and *Here is something beautiful.*

Wonder can be overwhelming. I know that I am seeing just a fraction of the world around me, and that there is far more that I'm missing. To be open to it, and to recognize what I can, including my ignorance of what I cannot see—that is the beginning of the awe-filled wonder that icons invite me toward.

Icons, it is said, are not painted but written. One who makes icons is called an icon writer. These are strange terms, but they connote the truth that the person making the image isn't representing something to us as much as opening a field of meaning. As Madeleine L'Engle puts it, "A true icon is not a reflection; it is a metaphor." While Michelangelo might picture a biblical scene, an iconographer works not to show us the scene but to open a door through which we can enter it. Such doors can take many forms. As L'Engle recounts, an Antarctic encounter with penguins proved to be such a door. "It is not flippant for me to say that a penguin is an icon for me," she writes, "because the penguin invited me to look through its odd little self and on to a God who demands of us that we be vulnerable as we open ourselves to intimacy, an intimacy which leads not only to love of creature, but to love of God." Any object of attention that invites our vision to the wider world beyond it is a kind of icon.

I've never written an icon, but I have drawn birds. I remember one day, as a teenager, watching a hawk circle over Holla Bend. There was something different about it. I had no camera, so I opened my National Geographic field guide and began to sketch the bird in the blank of the front flap. I went from the bird to the sketch, a basic outline where I tried to render the unique marks of the soaring raptor, watching-drawing-watching in a cycle. This, I became convinced over the long gaze of looking, was a Ferruginous Hawk, a very rare species. My sighting was, in fact, the second time this bird had ever been confirmed in the state.

Field sketching, though I have only done it sporadically, has given me a way to see birds, to attend to them in a more focused way than simply careful looking. There's no better way to clue in on a bit of plumage, or the shape of a bird, than to try to render it by hand on a piece of paper. I'm no accomplished bird artist, but I do return to working on my sketches, especially when I can hold myself back from hurry and linger with the birds before me, contemplating them rather than consuming them as check marks on a list. Perhaps one day I'll fill a bird notebook like Amy Tan's *Backyard Bird Chronicles*—her illustrations and notes written as joyful icons of the birds in her home landscape.

Recently we had a record snowfall in my city, one that closed our streets for days. I worked from home, sitting by a back window. I had spread birdseed on top of the snow on the back steps, just outside the window. A group of Dark-eyed Juncos gathered, many coming right up to the glass. It was a unique chance to see these birds in detail without needing binoculars.

As I sat by the window, I took to sketching the juncos. I wasn't making art. Just as an iconographer tries to "write" the holy through an image, I was attempting to take notes on the birds I was watching through tracing the lines of their bodies, shading in their colors. In this act of drawing, it wasn't the final sketch that was important. Instead, drawing was a way to force my attention toward this particular bird before me, an attention that was almost like seeing the bird anew. Each bird was no longer simply a "Dark-eyed Junco." Instead, through this sustained looking, I was beginning to see individuals, unique members of a flock.

At its best, drawing is a form of contemplation. It requires a striping away of what would normally be considered sight. Some years ago, I became friends with a visiting artist at a nearby university. I mentioned that I wanted to learn to draw, and he offered me some lessons. I purchased the sketch book he told me to get, the slender sticks of vine charcoal, the putty erasers. Sitting at his desk, he explained that the first task of drawing was to see shapes without turning them into objects—everything was to become lines and shadows, the identity of the thing was stripped away. An apple, for instance, must cease to be an apple. It was now just curves, lines, and shades of light. By simply drawing those lines, trying to replicate the light and dark, I would be able to produce a better rendering of the apple than if I consciously tried to draw my notion of an "apple."

So it is with a junco, or a cardinal, or any bird that might be so familiar that we simply pass them. It's easy to recognize or count an object without really seeing it. But contemplation, which is what any icon is meant to invite, beholds each reality before it as it is, in its essence, a realization of the wonder of every wing, the blazing red of a cardinal, the dark eye of the junco as it looks back with an intelligence in what can only be called recognition.

This contemplative stance is important because it helps us move into the infinite wholeness that lies behind every creature. To contemplate a cardinal isn't simply to know its species but to in some way know *it*, on a different level. In the early centuries of Christianity, philosophers sought to understand the nature of knowing. One form they labeled *curiositas*, which was a kind of learning that reduced the known to a mere object. This kind of knowledge was meant to be avoided. Instead, students were called to *contemplatio*—to take this stance of knowing in which subject and object disappeared. The outside was, in some way, brought inside.

I confess that I have often pursued birds as objects; I have birded for the sake of curiosity. I admit to jumping in my car and driving two hours to "get" a rare bird, then moving on as soon as the check mark dried or eBird record was submitted. If I had not been in the carload of people who found it, the Fork-tailed Flycatcher could easily have been such a bird.

But as I've grown older, I long more and more for the contemplative path. When I can enter that place, then I encounter even an Eastern Phoebe, a common flycatcher in my neighborhood, with the kind of wonder I had at that first Fork-tailed (though, I admit, still not with the rush of adrenaline).

Have you ever lingered with that strange thrush with an orange belly and white and black malar stripe? It cocks its head, seemingly listening to the grass. What is it hearing? Then, in an instant, the answer comes—a red worm is suddenly beneath the dark edges of its beak.

Where does this American Robin go when it is not in my yard? How many of its children wander the neighborhood, a common delight in the everyday world? To dwell, to attend to the world, this is the entry point for contemplation. And from that contemplation comes love: Love for birds and, with them, for the places they live.

Love is patient, love is kind, and it is dangerous. Love fosters the fierce desire to protect, which has always saved the world. Such saving does not happen, however, unless our eyes have been opened. An icon invites us to enter the gaze of affection that draws us toward the only action that really matters.

2

FEBRUARY

Liturgy

I HELD TIGHTLY to the handlebars of the mountain bike, my hands padded with two pairs of gloves—first, a light cotton blend, second a pair insulated with Gore-Tex for winter cycling, bright in neon yellow. Despite them, the tips of my fingers were growing numb as I worked to guide the wheels around ice patches and down the treacherous hills that dot my neighborhood to the east.

On my back was a pack containing 75 percent of my most valued earthly possessions. There was the bag itself, a Chrome backpack that is the most perfect and durable I've ever owned. Inside its front flap were my Zeiss binoculars, 10x42 with "Made in Germany" emblazoned on the dial. Within the main compartment of the roll top, I had my Swarovski spotting scope, padded in green with its "Habicht" emblem of a Northern Goshawk. These are tools I plan to use for the rest of my birding days, optics whose quality can hardly be improved upon.

I'm not much for consumerism, but as I learned from the theologian William Cavanaugh, really valuing a material thing can, somewhat ironically, be the exact opposite of a consumerist life. Consumerism relies on the here-today, replaced-tomorrow mindset. Loving the particular tools we use to engage the world is an ancient thing, and a good one. Which is all to say that I was doing my best not to crash the bike and break any of them.

My city had been hit with a record-breaking freeze, with days on end of temperatures never cresting above the single digits. Along with the cold we'd had snow, a layer several inches thick. The cold and the snow were not normal, but the weather never is these days. We went from an unusually warm winter to an Arctic blast—a pattern that's becoming more common as the climate changes. Our normally mild, even-keeled winters are now regularly interrupted by cold fronts pushed down from a warmer Arctic. The result is broken pipes and uncleared roads in a region where we used to consider it lucky to see a single dusting of snow.

The cold had been so unrelenting that many lakes in the area had frozen, not solid enough for ice skating but enough to shut many ducks out of their winter feeding grounds. As a result, they had headed to the Arkansas River, whose currents kept the water mostly clear.

And since the ducks were headed to the river, so was I.

Winter has always been among my favorite seasons for birding. Arkansas plays host to a wide variety of northern birds, from the ducks that make Arkansas an international destination for hunters to the orange-faced, elusive LeConte's Sparrows that run along the ground through the golden winter stands of Little Bluestem grasses. It is also the time of year when rare birds show up. From its gulls to its raptors, winter is a time of wandering.

Birding is a way to enter the rhythm at the heart of the world. No place, temperate or tropical, exists in a stasis—things change in a regular pattern over the course of our spinning journey around the sun. Rainy and dry, cold and warm, nesting and wintering, basic and alternate, planting, growing, harvesting—there are changes to the seasons, and we are part of them. And yet for most of us who live and work in an urban place, daily life is tied to the monotony of machines, the seasons disconnected from the wild clocks that work to keep the rhythm of the world. The school year and the fiscal year have become more basic to our existence than the natural cycles of our place. Yet the seasons are still within us, even if they have become abstracted.

I am a Christian priest in the Anglican tradition. Because of this, my work is marked by a different pattern of time, not necessarily rooted in creation but not apart from it either. It is sacred time, a way of counting the seasons reflected in the events of Christ's life, and the life of the church. The year begins not in January but with the first Sunday of Advent. It's a season marked by the color blue—a new dawn, the color of Mary, the mother of Jesus. Then there is the white of Christmas—a whole season, not a day—and then green, then purple, then white, and then green again, each color marking a new time of emphasis and imagination.

These seasons with their colors are a part of the liturgy. Often mistakenly translated as "the work of the people," the Latin origin of the word *liturgy* means something closer to "a public work." In the ancient world, a well-to-do patrician would build a road or put in an aqueduct for the sake of the people. Christians came to use the term for the pattern of their prayers, their way of marking the sacredness of space and time. These too, they believed, were a way of doing a public work—a way of making a new reality for the good of all.

The Eastern Orthodox theologian John Chryssavgis writes that liturgy is a reflection of the pattern of an icon. "The world of the icon," he writes, "offers new insights into reality. It reveals the eternal dimension in everything that we experience." Liturgy, this rhythm of seasons and rituals, for Chryssavgis, plays a similar role. "What an icon does with matter, the liturgy does with time," he writes. In liturgy, the "eternal dimension" finds its place within the rhythms of finite clocks and changing seasons.

For Chryssavgis, liturgy, in its life and practice, becomes more than mere ritual. Instead, it is "a commemoration of [the] innate connection between God and people and things. It is a celebration of the sense of communion; it is a dance of life." Dances are works of space and time, each marked by a rhythm. I know that dance through the liturgies of the church, but if I'm honest, I know the dance of life better through watching birds.

Birds do not follow mechanical clocks or printed calendars. They live by the sun, the earth's shifting tilt, the abundance of insects and the strategies of survival. To watch them is to move from the monotony of machine time, with its endless adherence to the beat of production, to the flow of life with all its ups and downs, its joy and grief, its abundance and scarcity—each an aspect of the world in its goodness.

I made it across the frozen blacktop, past a row of storage units and a business center where gyms are mixed with interior design firms and electricians' shops. In the corner of the parking lot there's an alley that runs along the river's side. A sandbar had formed by a small inlet where Rose Creek, the stream that is at the center of my neighborhood's watershed, pours into the Arkansas River. To come here is to arrive at a joint in the body of my life, the place where whatever runs from my yard, good or bad, joins in the waters of the river, which then moves toward the Mississippi and finally the Gulf. Permaculturalist Brock Dolman calls watersheds our "basin of relations." It is a way in which we can trace, through one ecological thread, how our small place in the landscape is connected to the whole.

In the protected waters of the bay were hundreds of birds: cormorants and gulls, ducks and pelicans. None of these birds are year-round residents. They are winter birds who will travel north to breed and nest and raise their young. Many of the birds I would see here in the summer—the orioles that nest along the river in the cottonwood trees, the Indigo Buntings that sing from the brushy edges—are now far south in Mexico and Central America. Like water, birds can be seen as connectors of places through time. To trace their patterns of migration and flight, their paths through flyways, is to see something like rivers of birds, streams of them.

To see these rivers in action, you can tune into a feed of live, unfiltered radar during the first weekend of May or the middle of September. The website BirdCast (birdcast.info) can make this easy, but any unfiltered radar feed will do. What you will see, in those glowing images, is a mass of birds flowing across the country, following the invisible channels of the major flyways—Atlantic, Mississippi, Central, and Pacific. During peak nights, the flow of birds will reach into the billions as they move from south to north in the spring and again north to south in the fall. Go outside and cup your ears toward the sky, and you just might hear flight calls as the birds move high above, forming their river of feathers over the landscape.

Rivers have also been a long-running metaphor for time. Like water, time has a flow to it. This flow can represent change, a constant shifting. When the ancient Greek philosopher Heraclitus sought a way to illustrate the unrepeatable instances that make up the world, he chose a river: "You can never cross the same river twice."

Yet there is also an aspect of that flow, changing as it is, that is eternal. At the end of Cormac McCarthy's apocalyptic novel *The Road*, after the world has been destroyed by a nuclear holocaust, McCarthy turns to a stream to offer a note of hope for enduring life after all of the novel's catastrophes. "Once there were brook trout in the streams in the mountains," he writes. "They smelled of moss in your hand. Polished and muscular and torsional. On their backs were vermiculate patterns that were maps of the world in its becoming. Maps and mazes. Of a thing which could not be put back. Not be made right again. In the deep glens where they lived all things were older than man and they hummed of mystery." For McCarthy's story of nuclear wasteland, a planet undone by human recklessness, it is fish in a hidden stream that signal the possibility of something more than the devastation wrought. What happened cannot "be made right again," and no return is possible. But still there courses a mystery, a watery one, that transcends the devastation.

This storm, the strange weather of the winter, the strange shifting of every season now, marks a slower undoing than a nuclear blast, but it too is a reality that cannot be made right. What we have done to the planet in this industrial era will be etched in the layers of sediment as long as the earth lasts, the Anthropocene having become an era in geologic time.

And yet, here, channeled and dammed and controlled as they are—the streams and rivers continue their flow. The birds return. Life continues its dance, even in the ruins.

As I had hoped, the river was filled with birds. Ring-billed Gulls circled, calling, as a small group of diminutive Bonaparte's Gulls cruised purposefully along the surface before breaking suddenly for a coordinated dive into the chilled water. In addition to the usual Mallards, the males with their iconic green heads, and the Gadwalls, elegant in their gray with black, there were Buffleheads, crisp with white and black, and on the shore a group of Green-winged Teal, a twist of broad green behind the eye on the cinnamon-colored heads of the males.

On the sandbar, where I can usually find a dozen Ring-billed Gulls, there were now hundreds of gulls, Ring-billed and Bonaparte's, joined by a couple of the less common Herring Gulls. The Bonaparte's Gulls were mostly white, with a black dot behind their ear. This is their basic plumage, the one I know because I have mostly encountered them on their wintering grounds. In the spring they will molt, changing out their worn winter feathers for new ones. It isn't simply a refresh, though. Adults will have a new color pattern, a head covered in a striking black.

At one time the plumages of birds like these February Bonaparte's would have been labeled "winter" plumage in many bird guides. Winter, it was recognized, is a relative term. Many species live in a kind of everlasting summer, moving from the northern to the southern hemisphere. What marks time for them isn't winter and summer but basic and breeding plumages—or as the ornithological language has developed it, "basic" and "alternate" plumages.

Birds in their movements and plumages are the markers of time changing, seasons coming and going. This is the time the ancient Greeks called *chronos*—personified by an old man with a beard. Chronos time is the sort that marches and moves, that clicks by in a circle on a clock. But there is another kind of time. This time is *kairos*. Kairos is that time that marks the right moment, the "opportune time." Kairos time is the place in which the earthly intersects with the heavenly, the time-bound and the eternal linked in a moment that steps out from the cycles of the clock.

There is something of this kairos reality in the practice of the Sabbath—the Jewish day on which work is set aside and delight has free play. In the idea of the Sabbath, time is unbound from simple progress and productivity; it stands outside the normal clicking, ticking measures. Claiming that God took a day of rest after the creation of the cosmos, and called on people to do the same, gives time a different quality. While other ancient Near Eastern creation myths claimed that humans were made as slaves for the gods, the biblical creation story calls on human life to follow the same pattern as God's life. Since God rested on the seventh day, human beings are to do the same.

But what was this time of rest? Was it merely a cessation of production and work, or was it something else? This was a question many ancient rabbis pondered and debated. They concluded that there *was* something, after all, that God made on the Sabbath. It was not a thing, another object of the universe, but instead a way of being. On the seventh day of creation, God created *menuha*: a deep delight in the world. This was the crowning moment of God's creation—wonder at the wild world.

Most of us, whether religious or secular, can glean some sense of the Sabbath reality from snow days. Suddenly, with little warning, all our obligations disappear, and we are free to be with friends, to enjoy the wild world around us, and to delight in the fun of fresh snow on the ground. I remember one night, soon after Emily and I were married, when we were invited into this time out of time. We lived in the same house we do now and, at the time, a number of our friends lived within a few blocks. With no one able to drive, a friend invited everyone to walk over for a potluck. Emily and I trudged through the snow, carrying a pot of chili, the five blocks to their house. The dark came fast, but with the snow and streetlamps, all was alight with a soft glow. This was a weekday, but none of us were worried about work or the rush of activities because everything had been canceled. We simply delighted in this moment together.

I wonder, watching birds, if they inhabit some kind of eternal sabbath. It was to them, after all, that Jesus pointed for an example of a life free of worry about the future: "Look at the birds of the air; they neither sow nor reap nor gather into barns, and yet your heavenly Father feeds them" (Matthew 6:26).

Do birds simply live "in the moment"? The research is mixed. Crows have been documented memorizing the schedule of trash pickups in neighborhoods, so that they know which neighborhoods to visit on which days. And chickadees, among a number of other birds, are great at caching seeds in thousands of places for those days when food is hard to find. Not to discount the wisdom of Jesus in "not storing up in barns," but some birds certainly do store up.

That said, birds are present to their place in time in a way we humans often are not. We let the power of our desires, our manipulation of the world, make time into a thing we try to manage, if not control. Instead of letting the sun and stars rule our days and nights, we flip switches. We attempt to command our own small cosmos, illuminating it with lights of our own making, usually to the detriment of the health of the world and us alike.

I'm writing these words late in the day. Most days I use the morning for my writing, but the day got away from me. A book doesn't get finished unless words get typed, sentences stacked upon one another. I've always preferred the layering of daily accumulations to a mad effort to get it all finished in a rush. So I'm here, in my writing shed, thinking of birds and time as the sun is beginning to set, my window facing west toward a rose-hued horizon edging into black.

Beside the shed is my chicken run and coop where my family keeps four Orpington hens. I can hear them, despite the insulation of the shed, and I know from their sounds that they are entering their coop for the night, obeying the sunset. With shorter days, the chickens have mostly ceased laying eggs. Among the four of them, I've been finding one egg every other day. Their egg production is tied to seasonal signals, including light exposure. The circadian rhythm of chickens is influenced by their pineal gland, which has photoreceptor cells that respond to the amount of light and length of day. Commercial egg-laying farms keep their chickens laying eggs all winter long by never turning out the lights, and even some farmstead operations put lights in coops to keep the eggs coming. The result of increased egg production through these lights is usually a shorter life for the hen. Though chickens are a thoroughly domesticated bird, there is still something of wild time within them. Their bodies are still tied to the seasons.

I do not use artificial lights to disrupt the natural rhythms of my chickens, and yet I sit here with an electric lamp turned on and a laptop's glowing screen illuminating my face. My life, like that of most humans in the modern world, has fallen out of rhythm with the natural patterns of time. I keep hours dictated more by the clock than by the sun, subjecting my body to a relentless demand for production that I refuse to make my chickens follow. My body has become disconnected from the greater rhythms of life, and like so many, it is suffering because of it.

Technology critic Lewis Mumford, in his now-classic 1934 book *Technics and Civilization*, places the blame for our machine-dominated world on the ordering of life in the Benedictine monasteries of the Middle Ages. The Benedictines, a monastic tradition that began in the early sixth century, followed a pattern of prayer called "the hours." These hours interrupted the day seven times, with the monks stopping their normal activity to gather for prayer, usually rooted in the Psalms. It was a literal and embodied practice of Psalm 119, verse 164: "Seven times a day do I praise thee."

This pattern of prayer was all well and good until the desire for regulating its practice led to the innovation of the clock. It was from the monasteries' interest in creating a uniform way of marking time that the modern clock was born. And with it, life began to be set to a rhythm not marked by the natural patterns of light and dark but by the clicking gears of a machine. Such a new, human-controlled means of keeping time resulted in the rise of capitalism and industry, and with them the world-transforming era we know as the Anthropocene. As Mumford writes, "one is not straining the facts when one suggests that the monasteries . . . helped to give enterprise the regular collective beat and rhythm of the machine; for the clock is not merely a means of keeping track of the hours, but of synchronizing the actions of men." Mumford goes on to write that the clock "is the key-machine of the modern industrial age."

While we may be in a postindustrial economy in which microchips are more important than steam engines, Mumford's insight still rings true. It is by the clock that we work and live, and that clock keeps us off balance with the natural patterns of time to which our bodies, like the bodies of birds, are tied.

My bike was propped against the metal guard rail of the parking lot, a barrier to keep inattentive drivers from careening down the riprap to the river. I swung my tripod from the inlet to the east and aimed my scope across the river to the north. With my binocular scan, I could see some ducks bobbing in the water, but they were too far away to identify with any certainty.

There's a second nature you can develop with binoculars or a birding scope. From years of practice, I can line up my sight and the scope and "get on a bird" quickly. I am adept with only a few physical tools, so this one is especially satisfying. It reflects a long history, a relationship between me, the tool, and the world I use it to explore.

What we do with our bodies and our minds, repeated in patterns over time, changes them. That's an obvious enough truth, and yet it is one that we often ignore. Like Oscar Wilde's quip that we all have the faces we deserve by forty, the habits of our bodies become the postures with which we engage the world. Birding can become one such posture—a way of attending to the world through our flesh.

Across the river, I look at the ducks bobbing near the shore. As I suspected, they are a pair of Common Goldeneyes. The male has bright white sides, a head of iridescent green, and a bold white oval at the base of the bill. The head of the male often appears dark, the green requiring just the right light to see, but today the sun was shining just right through the clouds to show its deep verdant iridescence. Beside it was a female, beautiful in the more subtle tones of gray and brown. Both birds had their eponymous golden eye, visible even at the distance of a hundred yards.

One feature of our experience of time is how it draws and pulls upon our memories, our past experiences returning into the present. There's a theological term for this reality. It is called *anamnesis*: literally, a "recalling to mind." During the Christian liturgy of the Eucharist, there is a moment in which the work of God in history is remembered. This tradition draws on the Jewish prayers of the Passover, which retell the story of God's deliverance of Israel from their sojourn of slavery in Egypt. These are moments of *anamnesis*, a time in which the memory of what made this reality possible is brought into the present. Through their repetition, these stories, these memories, become more than history. By calling them to mind, we are recognizing the effects of the past that continue to live with and through us. Whether it is the history of life on the planet, reflected in each creature, or the ways of living given to us before we were born, history is our inheritance. The question is not how to let it go, but how to carry what we have been given and move with it into the future we want.

Watching these birds across the river brought me back to my early days of birding. I had a cheap scope then, one that distorted the light with prismatic rainbows around the edges but had just enough clarity to be useful at the center. One of my favorite places to go was a bay on the reservoir lake of our city. That was where I first saw Common Goldeneyes, out across the water near the lake's dam.

Not every species carries with it this kind of memory, but many do. A first encounter or an extraordinary moment with a species—those memories go deep within me and resurface every time I see that bird again. With a long history of watching, the world becomes etched with these memories, sparked by birds and the stories that go with them. An average walk through a local park can be like flipping through a photo album—memory upon memory ignited with each sighting.

These memories are important because they mark change. For as long as there have been birds, they have shifted their populations in response to a complex mix of conditions. Yet, now is a time of rapid change like no other, and with it the memory of what was, set against the reality of what is happening now. Spend time with a group of birders and you'll often hear them remark on these changes. Some birds, especially those who favor the warmer states to the south, have moved north. Others, those that prefer colder conditions, are hardly to be seen any more. I've never met a birder who doesn't believe in climate change. They can see its effects, even over the span of a few years.

To the west of the Goldeneye, just beyond the opposite side of the river, high sandstone cliffs are edged with pines at the top. These cliffs are the remnant of a quarry that once sent stone down the river. Now the quarry and the land above and below are part of a park. A cycling "pump track" lies below, a course where riders use momentum to ride up and down banks without peddling. Above are walking trails and vistas of the whole river valley. The cliffs themselves offer vertical routes for rock climbers.

Looking at the cliff, I can see the layers that formed the hill, time etched foot by foot. Before birds caught my attention, I was interested in what lay on the ground and in it. I alternated between an interest in paleontology and archaeology, and fossils and artifacts from my childhood still fill many of my shelves. From those disciplines I learned another way of seeing time. We tend to think of time as lines plotted out in a series, but it can also come in layers. The past is stacked upon by the present, soon to be covered over by the future.

Among my fossils were the bones of dinosaurs, the most important ecological actors for millennia. Then something brought their end in a cataclysm—a moment of radical upheaval. But they did not disappear altogether. The dinosaurs that survived were those who'd taken to the trees, the ones who grew feathers. Karl Marx once wrote, "Human anatomy contains a key to the anatomy of the ape." It is easier, Marx meant, to look back to see where we have been than to look forward to where we are going. In birds, you can see dinosaurs in the rearview mirror.

Above the cliffs, Turkey Vultures tilted in the icy air. More than most birds, vultures bear the family resemblance to dinosaurs in their faces. But lines and layers are not enough to understand time. Both can create an alluring sense of progress, that all must come in stages, one succeeding the other. It is this narrative that pushes birds to the brink as they are "sacrificed" to a new stage of progress.

It was birds that fully awakened my ecological conscience. I had been raised in a wild place, and my father, a deep lover of trees, had communicated the tragedy of ever having to cut one. But it was in watching birds, and learning the intricate relationships they had with their supporting households of life, that I began to see the urgency of caring for the earth in all its many places.

Conservative talk radio was often playing in our car when I was a child, and I remember hearing Rush Limbaugh pontificating about the Spotted Owl, a species that lives in the old-growth forests of the western United States and Mexico. At the time, the owl was a rallying cry for conservationists opposed to the logging of old-growth forests in the Pacific Northwest, where the owls had lost well over half of their historic habitat. Limbaugh, I remember, avoiding the direct language of evolution, said that species must adapt to new conditions. If the owls couldn't change to survive in the world humans were making, then they'd just have to die off, he implied. I knew, even as a child, that this was foolish. I knew that we as humans were creating new conditions far too quickly, and that we owed something to these owls who had lived for centuries in these forests, long before the power of engines had enabled their rapid destruction.

Limbaugh's logic reflects a way of thinking that still reigns in much of American life, indeed in all the capitalist logics of the industrial world. Progress must be made, and all those who can't keep up—be they cultures, places, animals, or ecosystems—must fall to the wayside. There are versions of this on the left and the right, both with their own views of progress, be it economic or social or both. In either case, the gifts of what is here—the given life of the world as it is, with ancient trees and owls that nest in them—is not valued.

The result is that even as we face the upheavals of climate disaster, the only imagination we have is of a new form of progress, albeit a green one. Solar panels will be our salvation, zero-carbon machines our messiah. It is easy to imagine such possibilities from the confines of a desk and a screen, a couch and a television. But standing beside the river with its frozen edges, each breath made crystalline in the air before me and birds rotating above the water, I know that it will not do. We must make room for a different kind of reality, not one tied to the narratives of progress but a whole new way of life.

This winter storm, one that broke records, was not a normal happening in a long line of time. It was an event, an upheaval. For seasons to continue in the long dance of their ancient rhythms, with the migrations of birds, the hatching of insects, the blooming of flowers, and a thousand other events all happening in a synchronized dance of life, then humans need to embrace this as a moment of kairos. Chronos, in its most ancient form and dance, needs kairos to continue.

There is a third form of time for the Greeks. Chronos marks the time that passes, kairos is the opportune time, and *krisis* is the moment when things change and turn. The famous Greek doctor,

Hypocrites, used this last word to describe the point when a disease broke either toward health or death. *Krisis* is the inflection point, and how we live into kairos can make the difference for its direction. We must decide how we will act in this moment. How will we answer the crisis before us?

Few now disagree that we live in a time of ecological upheaval. It is, as many say, a crisis. And yet, this is also a moment of kairos—the opportune time to welcome a new reality. Usage of the word *kairos* has been on the rise in recent years. A look at the Google "Ngram Viewer," which displays usage trends of words in books, shows a sharp rise in the use of *kairos* in the 2000s. Searching for a word to express this moment, many of us are increasingly reaching for *kairos*. It is the opportune time, the moment to embrace a different way of life.

I hear a rattle off to my right, at the edge of the inlet. A Belted Kingfisher, blue with a band of orange on its belly flies low over the water. *Megaceryle alcyon* is the Latin name for this species. *Alcyon* is a name drawn from the Greek goddess Halcyon. There is a myth that this goddess, the daughter of the god of wind, was to be married to a human king, Ceyx. In bed one night, the two pretended that they were Zeus and Hera, an act of hubris which angered Zeus. He sent punishment upon them. When Ceyx went on a voyage, his ship sunk and he was drowned. Just before he drowned, he begged Poseidon to bring his body to his wife. At the same time, Halcyon begged the supreme goddess Hera for mercy. In the end, the call of mercy won the hearts of the gods. The couple still had to suffer for their hubris, but as an allowance they were turned into kingfishers so they could continue to live together. However, because they were forced to live at the edge of the water, it was difficult for them to nest. Just as soon as they built a nest and laid eggs in it, flood waters would rise and destroy it. Again, mercy won out and the gods set a time in the midst of the winter when the pair of kingfishers were given just enough calm to raise their chicks. These periods became known as Halcyon days.

The myth of Halcyon and Ceyx being turned into kingfishers is a story of hubris and love. It was hubris that led to the couple's woes, and yet despite their hubris there was still real love between them. It was that love that brought them the mercy of the gods, an allowance amid their punishment, just enough good days to keep life going.

The waters are rising because of our hubris, our betrayal of the boundaries of the given world. The question is whether we can cultivate the love to bring mercy amid the destruction we've brought. Will we be granted enough Halcyon days to welcome the continuation of life in the midst of the storms of our unraveling climate? Watching the kingfisher glide above the water, I am hopeful for such a time.

After an hour by the river, the protective layers of my winter clothes began to give way to the cold. My hands were numb, my lips chapped by the wind. I packed up my scope and binoculars and swung my pack to my back. I rode along the river as I made my way back home, seeking gentler slopes to climb back up from the valley. As the day began to fade, I was filled with love for all those birds swirling around the river, and I was grateful for this time to be with them, even at a distance. "Time is the revealer of love," wrote the Catholic theologian Hans Urs von Balthasar. "Time is God's most glorious invention, as revelation of his patience (because there is always more Time) and of his impatience (because Time is irreversible)."

It is in that place of love, between patience and impatience that we stand, invited toward the dance of life and the work of keeping the ancient rhythms going.

3

MARCH

Hospitality

AS FEBRUARY TURNED to March, sewage began spilling from our bathtub drain. We called a rooter service, but after a few hours the man, sweating, came back to say that clearing the line was beyond his abilities. In fact, during his attempt, our sewer pipe had broken, and we now had waste pooling in our backyard. We'd need a plumber and probably a new sewer line.

Our sewer line, it turns out, was not made of the strong stuff of ceramic or steel but was instead built of bitumen and wood pulp, a material called Orangeburg pipe. After nearly a century, the weight of the soil and the waning integrity of the pipe had resulted in the line being flattened into a shape closer to a football than a cylinder.

We checked our savings account, called a plumbing company, and got on their schedule for the following Monday. Early that morning, at 7 a.m. sharp, I stood in my driveway with the backhoe operator, talking through the best plan of action for digging out our line. The birds were singing their morning chorus, flying this way and that in the trees above.

I can sometimes find it difficult to carry on conversations outside. My wife has become accustomed to the fact that our morning coffee on the porch might be interrupted by an exclamation about a Yellow Warbler I just heard in the neighbor's yard or a Mississippi Kite dipping across the horizon. Others, less familiar and forgiving of my wandering attention, can get annoyed.

As I talked with the backhoe operator, just behind the man's head I caught a sight of motion on the horizon. It was a raptor of some kind, holding its wings in a "V" like a Turkey Vulture but with a slenderer build. My memory snapped to recognition—this was a Northern Harrier, a ghostly bird that hunts the open fields of Arkansas through the winter. I saw it for a mere second before it was gone, but it was enough. With his backhoe churning in idle, the man didn't seem to notice my distraction.

I'd never seen a harrier from my yard, as our neighborhood is hardly the right habitat. This bird was likely traveling from one field to another or beginning its migration north, taking a shortcut across the city. Still, it counted as a new species for my yard list—a tally of all the species I've seen in or from my small urban plot. As I entered my sighting into eBird, I realized that this harrier was the hundredth species for our place—a great total for any yard, especially one in the city.

Keeping a yard list is a common birder's pursuit, sometimes the first foray into listing. Lists are an important part of birding for many. At their best they can serve as an album of encounters with the diverse wonders of the winged world. Some birders go to great lengths to build extensive lists of all the birds they've seen over their lifetime. I've known a few who will jump on a plane at the first mention of a rare bird to add to their life list. There are an estimated ten thousand species of birds in the world, and there are birders who have spent years of their lives and thousands of dollars to see over 90 percent of them. Others stick to listing in the continental United States or the American Birding Association (ABA) Area, which includes everything north of the US border with Mexico up to the Arctic, and more recently the Hawaiian Islands. Birders often also keep year lists, state lists, county lists, heard-only lists, seen-only lists: only the imagination is a limit for the variety of ways birders catalog their encounters with birds.

For all the globe-trotting that keeping a life list of birds can involve, nothing is simpler than counting what shows up in your yard. It can be a way to train your focus and attention; a path to wondering at the diversity right where you are. But to reach one hundred species is the result not just of watching and identifying what happens to fly by. Reaching a hundred species, at least in this part of the world, marks the fruit of hospitality, the creation of a gathering place for the diversity of life.

Bird feeders can help with this hospitality. As a boy, I filled our yard with different kinds of feeders, catering to a wide array of species. Now, though I still offer seed and suet in the winter and sugar water in the summer, I have increasingly put my efforts toward creating habitat rather than buying seed. Call it a locally grown buffet, fresh from the garden.

I have never been much for a traditional lawn—close-cropped grass with a few trees and shrubs spread out at wide intervals. I have box gardens for vegetables in the front yard and have long kept chickens in the back. But it was only after decades of birding that I began to catch a vision of creating habitat where I live. By thinking about my small patch of ground differently, I have come to see that I can provide a haven for migrating birds, a home for the year-around residents, all by carefully planting the right mix of plant species.

My wife, Emily, never says "our house"; instead, she calls this place "our home." It's an important choice of words. A house is a kind of building, whereas a home is a dwelling place. *Home* comes from an Old English word, *ham*, from which we also get our word *hamlet*. Like hamlet, that original word referred to villages as much as single homes—a dwelling place for a community as much as a family.

I like this root, for it can instruct us in a different way of understanding our place. Every home is a site of dwelling for a community, both within and without. In biologist Rob Dunn's book *Never Home Alone*, he traces the diverse forms of life that share our human habitations—the kinds of fungi that take up residence in our bathtub drains, and the camel crickets that prefer our crawl spaces and basements. Some may cringe at such a shared life, but Dunn shows that it is simply a part of our reality as creatures on a shared planet. And while the species Dunn profiles have a particular preference for human homes, we can turn the consciousness of our shared space toward the deliberate work of hospitality for nonhuman creatures.

Hospitality, in the Christian understanding, is at the heart of all existence, the creation itself. Nothing exists of necessity, all is an extravagance—a gift of the God who made room for the creation. Simone Weil, the mystic philosopher of World War II–era France, reflected this in one of her essays on the reality of creation. "On God's part creation is not an act of self-expansion," she wrote, "but of restraint and renunciation." There is much to unpack here, more than a book on birds can afford, but Weil's insight is that creation is the result of making room—a place was created where no place had been before.

The human creature, in the Genesis story, is made in the image of God. What if part of what that means is that we too are meant to make room—that part of being fully human is to open up space for other creatures? Genesis 1 also famously gave "dominion" over the earth to human beings, which has justified all sorts of exploitation. But such dominion, at least in the English translation, could be read as one who makes a domicile. What if our call isn't to lord it over creation but to be a host?

If that is the case, then we have been failing miserably. The world is dominated by human activity. Just take to the air, like a bird, and you can see it. On a recent trip to Chicago, I looked down from the descending jet at the Midwestern landscape. For miles I saw nothing but agricultural fields and human settlements. Only along the creeks that ran like veins through the landscapes was there any real space for wildlife, trees forming a buffered riparian zone. And soon both the fields and the creeks faded to the solid swath of concrete that is the city.

It is as Gerard Manley Hopkins said in his poem of creation, "God's Grandeur":

> *Generations have trod, have trod, have trod;*
> *And all is seared with trade; bleared, smeared*
> *with toil;*
> *And wears man's smudge and shares man's smell:*
> *the soil*
> *Is bare now, nor can foot feel, being shod.*

"And for all this," he continues, "nature is never spent; / There lives the dearest freshness deep down things."

Over the world Hopkins sees the Holy Spirit as a bird, brooding, with "bright wings," nurturing life despite our destruction. When I arrived in Chicago and walked through the concrete streets, I saw a Peregrine Falcon darting among the skyscrapers, happy to feed on the easy prey of Rock Pigeons. In a pocket park, with hardly a half dozen trees, I heard the sound of Black-capped Chickadees making a life at the edge.

This is not to say that all will survive or thrive. But if we offer a little space, creation will come and fill it. It is our work to make more space.

Offering space for hospitality was something I began in earnest after reading Douglas Tallamy's books, *Bringing Nature Home* and *Nature's Best Hope*. I knew that planting a berry bush would help to attract fruit-eating birds, that an oak could provide a place for nesting, but it was not until I read Tallamy that I began to understand the whole network of life that could be welcomed by choosing just the right plants.

Tallamy is an entomologist, which might seem make him a strange choice to dispense bird-habitat advice, except that birds eat a lot of insects. In fact, even if the adults are primarily seed eaters, most species of birds rely on insects for feeding their young. Insects, especially those invertebrates like caterpillars that are particularly important for birds, eat plants. But not just any plant will do. Plants work to fend off pests by becoming toxic to most invertebrates. A select few invertebrates, however, have adapted to tolerate the poisons of a specific plant. The result is that if we want to have caterpillars so that we can support birds, then we must include in our landscaping the kinds of plants caterpillars can eat. And given that these relationships were forged over millennia, native plants that have coevolved with native insect species are the best.

I first got a lesson in these kinds of relationships one late summer day several years back. My friend Bill Shepherd, a retired botanist in his seventies at the time, had come by to pick me up for a birding trip to a local wildlife refuge. When he saw a bright orange butterfly in my yard, he commented, "Oh, that's a Gulf Fritillary! You must have some Passion Vine nearby."

At that time I didn't know a Gulf Fritillary from a Passion Vine, but soon after Bill pointed them both out to me, I realized that the plant grew everywhere around my yard. If I had been focused on a traditionally landscaped yard, I would have considered the plant a weed. And yet, as I began to identify it, I also started to notice orange caterpillars with black spikes crawling along it, taking bites from the leaves. Then I started to notice small yellow eggs on some of the undersides of the leaves. The Passion Vine is the host plant for Gulf Fritillary butterflies, which depend on it for fostering a new generation. By having it in my landscape, I was playing host to the host plant.

Passion Vine has a very specific host plant relationship with Gulf Fritillaries, but some plants, like oak trees, are host to hundreds of species of caterpillars for moths and butterflies. It was no wonder, I began to realize, that my neighbor's large Red Oak was always a good spot to look for migrating warblers each spring. The warblers were seeking out the caterpillars that were feeding on the tree's leaves.

These native plants have developed host relationships with insects in a way that non-native plants have not. Ornamental trees like Japanese maple and ginkgo, though beautiful, do not provide hospitality for most native caterpillar species. Because of this, they do not provide all that much food value to birds either. It has become Tallamy's mission to return the landscaping around our homes to native plants that support a local ecological community. In that way, our yards can all become part of the solution for preserving nature rather than continuing to take away space from wild creatures.

In *Nature's Best Hope*, Tallamy presents his vision for a network of native landscaping in yards and parks, as well as church, business, and school campuses, all working together to create corridors for wildlife. "Across the United States, millions of acres now covered in lawn can be quickly restored to viable habitat by untrained citizens with minimal expense and without any costly changes to infrastructure," writes Tallamy. This effort is one that he calls "Home Grown National Park."

In a way, the Home Grown National Park is an inversion of the original idea of the National Park. For John Muir, who first called for the creation of such a system, parks were places free from human habitation, set aside for their extraordinary splendor. These were not what the farmer and essayist Wendell Berry calls "working landscapes." They were "wild places," envisioned as pristine and free from human life, except for those visitors who came to hike and go home. But of course, we know such divisions are rarely so simple.

There is no doubt a need for places free of human domination. We need extraordinary, wild habitats by which we can understand and model thriving and healthy landscapes. But when we turn our attention only to the wild, it can result in a kind of dichotomy in our souls, a division of the spirit.

I've known birders and backpackers who love the wild world and spend time and money pursing experiences in it. And yet the way they make their living, and the way they live their daily lives, stands in direct conflict with the continued wholeness of which those wild landscapes are a part. In his book *The Unsettling of America*, Wendell Berry sought to understand the roots of our ecological crisis. In a searing chapter, "The Ecological Crisis as a Crisis of Character," Berry began with the story of an exposé the *Los Angeles Times* did of several leading environmental organizations. As the newspaper revealed, these organizations had their endowments invested in the very environmentally destructive companies that they were fighting against. "The difficulty," Berry writes, "is that, although the investments were absurd, they were *not* aberrant; they were perfectly representative of the modern character. These conservation groups were behaving with a very ordinary consistency; they were only doing as organizations what many of their members were, and are, doing as individuals. They were making convenience of enterprises that they knew to be morally, and even practically, indefensible." We have a problem, it turns out, of integrity.

We can begin to heal that rift between our love and actions, our values and our daily lives, by turning our attention to whatever patch of ground we have been given to tend, even if it is a potted planter on a balcony in the city. This work becomes a way in which we can begin to build the skills and knowledge to care for our homes, not only our yards and interior spaces but those larger, shared home places of watershed and ecoregion.

When my wife and I moved to this house, the yard had a typical variety of species for our region. There was a large lantana shrub right off the porch, and my wife transplanted some calla lily bulbs that had come from her grandparents' house—a keepsake plant. Otherwise, the front yard was largely a weedy mess of grass, a mix of invasives from Europe and Asia. I then began to read about permaculture and found inspiration in the book *Gaia's Garden* by Toby Hemenway.

Permaculture began as a way of rethinking agriculture in an ecological mode. As its name would suggest, it is oriented toward a "permanent agriculture" as opposed to the conventional farming focus on annual plants. Rather than planting one species of plant, year after year, permaculture seeks to imitate natural patterns anchored in perennial systems with a variety of plants (annual and perennial), vines, trees, and animals all working in concert to create an ecological whole. *Gaia's Garden* showed us how to begin doing all of this on a home scale.

Emily and I planted a pear tree, accompanied by a yaupon holly and an elderberry shrub. By luck, two of those species were local to our area. We also planted cultivars of blackberries that, albeit thornless, fulfill some important ecological functions—not least of which is creating habitat for bumble bees to nest in the broken-off ends of the branches. Permaculture gave us the tools to think about a layered structure to our yard, patterned in the likeness of a forest. It was from there that we moved toward a landscape centered around native plants. Year by year, slowly, we have been adding more diversity, both in terms of species and structure. While we haven't removed our lantanas and calla lilies, we make sure that any new perennial plants in our yard are native to our region.

Some might call this work "rewilding." I'm not opposed to the term, but it can also obscure the critical role I'm playing in the landscape. This is not simply letting things go; already human interventions in the landscape have been too great for that. An overgrown empty lot doesn't provide the same opportunity for ecological diversity as a well-tended native plant landscape. I found a better term for what we're trying to do from Benjamin Vogt, a landscape designer who wrote the great practical guide to native plant gardening entitled *Prairie Up*. Vogt says that instead of rewilding, he prefers the term "reconciliation ecology." It doesn't have quite the same ring as rewilding, but it communicates an important difference. In reconciliation, the focus is on coexistence with the natural world and the human-built environment. It's not an all-or-nothing approach, but it can have a significant impact. Imagine a suburb with every lawn made up of a matrix of native grassland species. It would be a far more hospitable place for a variety of creatures than the current model of home landscape, which provides little more habitat than would astroturf.

My neighborhood is a laissez-faire kind of place. There are grandmothers with neat flower beds, retirees with more than one "project" car in the yard, disassembled in various states of repair, and well-meaning gardeners with box gardens that started as good ideas but ended as collections of weeds. This makes for a good place for me to do what I want with my home habitat. For those with fussier neighbors, Tallamy and Vogt provide plenty of examples of native plant yards that would fit in the most manicured of environments. As *The New York Times* has reported, in some places, native plants are becoming the in-vogue landscaping fashion. You could be a trendsetter.

Providing hospitality for wild creatures isn't just about plants, though. Habitats are also about gardening habits. Along our street runs a strip of native flowers and grasses. In the summer, in full bloom, they're a beautiful array of yellows and purples, greens and whites. But by November, they've all turned to a uniform brown—dry stalks standing in place of the flowers.

In traditional gardening, the fall is the time to "clean up" the garden—raking leaves, cutting off the dead stubble of the summer plants, and sending it all to the city composting facility. This cleaning up, however, empties the garden of an opportunity for winter hospitality. Just because the plants have let go of their life above ground doesn't mean that they aren't still providing important ecological support for the wild lives around them.

Those dead flower heads, for instance: They are full of seeds that birds can feed on through the winter months. Offering those seeds and letting them be spread by birds in the winter is part of the life cycle of the plant. Why cut it short by a misguided standard of a "tidy yard"?

Hospitality comes with compromises, of course. Sometimes a little trimming must be done. Still, I love to let the habitat I've grown over the summer continue its work through the winter, as seeds provide food and leaves offer hiding places for overwintering insects.

Just outside my writing shed there is a stand of Jerusalem artichokes I planted. A member of the sunflower family, this flower has stalks that grow tall while producing an edible tuber underground. Even after the flowers have faded, they provide a safe haven for birds, who can find protection from a hawk or a cat by hiding among the dead standing stalks. I often watch as White-throated Sparrows move through the stalks, shoving back the leaves in little jumps, searching for insects and seeds beneath the crumpled brown. The stalks give the sparrows safety from the Cooper's Hawks that often cruise my yard searching for prey, and the loose cats that sometimes make their way across the fence.

Leaves and stems left on the ground also provide a nursery for many insects. Whether eggs or pupa, many insects overwinter by hiding in plant stems or in the leaf litter. When we just rake it all up and put our yard "waste" by the curb in a plastic bag, we are disturbing the cycles of life that are seeking to fill our home landscapes with ever more variety and abundance. Who wouldn't want to provide a nursery for another generation of insects, especially when we remember that most are not in any way a pest to humans? Leaving the leaves could be as consequential for birds as feeding them seed through the winter, and probably even more so. To promote this truth, landscape designer Benjamin Vogt sells T-shirts with slogans like "Leave the Leaves" and "Leaves Aren't Litter." They're on my Christmas list.

The work of hospitality also includes caring for your guests and ensuring their safety. In March, a pair of American Robins built a nest in our catalpa tree, a towering hardwood that blooms with beautiful white flowers in the spring and hosts finger-sized catalpa hornworm caterpillars in the summer. I liked thinking about the interaction between bird, tree, and caterpillar—it represented everything I wanted my yard to offer.

Then one day in late March, I heard a hard thud on the back of our house. I knew what it was, and immediately ran back to see if there was any hope for the victim. A young robin, her breast speckled like the thrush she is, lay dead beneath the window, her neck snapped.

I felt terrible, because I knew better. I had read the reports from the American Bird Conservancy about the dangers glass poses to birds, and I'd participated in local Audubon Society forums about finding a solution. Whether large windows or small, if a bird sees what seems to be a clear path, they will attempt to fly through it. At this time of day, our back window was reflecting the blue sky and tree branches opposite it. This young robin hadn't had the chance to learn the difference.

Just as many small works of hospitality can meaningfully support birds, so can many small acts of carelessness lead to significant loss. Cats and windows are two of the worst culprits at the home scale. "My cat doesn't kill birds," many a person tries to explain, when letting their felines roam free from the house. Others just give a sheepish grin as they note the feathered "gifts" their cats drop on their porch (along with other wild creatures, from snakes to frogs). The cumulative damage of such killing, however, is massive.

The solution is relatively simple—keep pet cats indoors. One would never dream of letting dogs out to roam freely in a neighborhood; in fact, in most places it is illegal to do so. The same standard should be applied to cats. In the end it is better for the cat (indoor cats live longer) and better for the creaturely neighborhood.

Windows can be a harder problem. Our cat lived indoors for the last thirteen years of her life, but, as the fallen robin in my yard attests, only recently have I begun to address the window problem at my house. Windows, depending on the light, can be either reflective or invisible. Both create a problem for birds. Some, like the robin, die on impact. Many, however, fly away and die of internal injuries later, so homeowners never really see the damage done.

The solution is to provide something that makes the window visible to birds. Dark hawk silhouettes, as are often used, are insufficient. Instead, there needs to be a visible barrier every four inches. Smaller than that, and a bird might try to fly through. Birds, after all, are good at darting through small spaces.

ABC Bird Tape, which comes in strips or dots, helps provide a transparent covering for windows that make them visible for birds. Resembling thick Scotch tape, this bird tape is specially designed to be both transparent and reflect light in such a way that birds can see it. Another tried-and-true solution are Acopian Bird Savers. These are lengths of parachute cord you can hang like streamers across a window. They are available for purchase online or can be easily homemade. Some have even created mobile-like hangings with an artistic flair. There's a chance to be creative, as long as it fits the standard. More information can be found at the American Bird Conservancy's website.

Birds need a safe space where they can feed, drink, and live without a cat hiding in the bushes or a window hazarding their flight. As we think about hospitality for birds, we need to think about these things as an essential part of our work of hosting.

I have a friend who works to certify yards as wildlife friendly. She said that you can have all the right plants, water features, and other landscaping elements, but if you haven't done something about your windows or cats, then you haven't created a haven; you've set a trap. From hostile to hospitable—that's the work before us, a work that begins at home but moves beyond it.

March is when migration begins. After a winter of ducks and sparrows, sapsuckers and kinglets—all northern species that make Arkansas their winter home—the birds that went farther south begin their journey north again. The shorebirds are the first to arrive, many of them long-distance travelers that move from one pole of the globe to the other. For birders, the task is finding these migrants as they travel through. In inland states like Arkansas, shorebirds love the muddy fields where crustaceans can be picked from the clods. The drained ponds of fish farms are a favorite spot for many.

Near my home, the best place to go each March is an industrial park. The Port of Little Rock is a place where oil pipelines are built, steel is milled, and interstate signs are printed with their reflective sheen. Around a bend, an Amazon distribution center towers above the landscape, with a steady flow of cars, vans, and trucks bringing and taking items from the "everything store." On a good night, as I walk along the edge of one of the fields, I can smell the scent of roasting peanuts from the peanut-butter factory nearby.

That such a busy place of industry would be a good place for watching birds might seem odd. Yet the bend of the river that makes it a good industrial site also makes it a good stopover for species that have been traveling over this land far longer than any trucks or trains. Because industrial sites often require open spaces, cooling ponds, and other features that parallel the wild, they can preserve habitat that's lost in the urban core. What local birders simply call "the Port" has swampy forests, open grasslands, and flooded fields dotted among the factories. These bits of habitat, as fragmented as they are, have attracted a variety of species, ranging from a breeding population of Western Kingbirds that are east of their normal range to a Snowy Owl that wowed birders as it perched on windmill turbines one winter. I've seen more than 135 species in this place, and many are birds I could find nowhere else in my county.

One evening, headed to the Port for an end-of-day birding trip, I pulled up beside a field on Industrial Harbor Road. There is a quiet to a place like this in the waning hours, as though the rush and rumble of the day is answered by a balancing silence. This particular field is low-slung, just a few hundred yards from the river. A channel from the river runs into it, and there is often water pooled there during the rainy season. When the pond dries up, its edges are crusted with mud where flies lay larvae and crawfish pool. Shorebirds often gather at this edge, sometimes a handful, sometimes hundreds. On this evening, a single Pied-billed Grebe floated on the deeper waters.

The usual quiet, however, was broken. Floodlights had been set up at the water's edge, and dump trucks were rumbling past, a small bulldozer shoving their loads into the water. One truck passed, then another and another. As I drove around the bend, I saw a sign that read "KMC Trucks Only." It was the company that was working to demolish and expand a major interstate bridge nearby, and I realized that this was their fill site—the place they were going to dump the rubble. The Port, then, was using the rubble to fill in the field—a process that would destroy this wetland and remove one more stopover spot for migrants, one more winter feeding ground for ducks, one more field for the kingbirds and nesting meadowlarks. I felt a mix of grief, rage, and despair as I looked at the muddy expanse. Dump truck after dump truck came in, emptying their loads, the bulldozer pushing them toward the water.

When I got home, I wrote a lament to our Arkansas birders email list. It stirred a call to action. The bird conservation director of the regional Audubon center reached out to the Port's director, and we got a meeting.

The director, as well as several members of the Port board, were all outdoor enthusiasts. They spend their time off going to experience nature. But that nature was "out there," in special places like parks. They did not think about the places they drove by every day as habitats for wildness, even though Black-bellied Whistling Ducks gathered in the drainage ditch by the Amazon distribution center and Greater Yellowlegs could be seen wading in the retention pond by an empty warehouse. They needed a vision for the wild that was here, ready to accept whatever hospitality could be extended. To fail to see that wildness—to assume it was only elsewhere, pristine and removed—would be to continue to squeeze it out and exclude it from any plans.

Many years ago, I had the chance to hear a talk by the artist Alfredo Jaar. He is known for his large-scale consciousness-raising installations. In 1999, the city of Montreal invited Jaar to make use of the landmark Marché Bonsecours building. Jaar spent weeks walking the streets of Montreal, looking for inspiration for his installation. On one of his walks, he saw a hidden entryway. He followed it and realized it led to a homeless shelter. As he investigated, he came to see that homelessness was a major problem in Montreal, but that it was hidden from public view. The unhoused were not visible on the streets as they are in many cities. Jaar decided to, quite literally, shed light on the situation: He installed large lights in the Marché Bonsecours and connected them to buttons at the entrances of the city's shelters. He put a sign by the buttons telling those entering that if they wanted to let the city know of their presence, they should push the button. At night, as the city's unhoused poured into the shelters, the lights would strobe with a presence that had been hidden to that point. Jaar's installation invited the city of Montreal to a new recognition of those in need of hospitality all around them.

Birders can serve as flashing lights, making the world aware of the creatures they do not usually see and of the wild things in need of hospitality. As the birders in my community responded to the habitat loss at the Port, we also began a renewed effort to record the birds in the place. It had always been a popular place for birding, but now we recorded every bird with a new urgency. We wanted to show what could be lost or gained by how the land was managed.

Seeing no hope in picking a fight with a major economic development center for the city, our small group of birders sought collaboration. We found a good partner in the Port's director, a man who had once been a director of city parks. The bulldozing and infill couldn't be stopped, he told us, but a neighboring field would never be developed. If we wanted to, we could work to create an enhanced wetland there. We looked over a map of the Port and identified other places that would never be developed, each a marginal space limited by water, poor soil, and other factors that provided protection from the onslaught of industrial "progress." Of them all, a triangle-shaped field close to the one being filled in, showed the greatest promise. Perhaps by the time the existing wetland was lost, we'd have another, even better one right next to it, that could host migrating shorebirds, wintering ducks and sparrows, and nesting kingbirds and meadowlarks well into the future.

We went to work, reaching out to an ecological design firm that agreed to create a plan for the enhanced wetland. They put together a design for channeling water into the field, planting native wetland species, and developing an edge-of-wet-prairie habitat. Unlike the field that relied on the native powers of nature to carve out a space, this field would be carefully designed and enhanced—restoring far more than letting it go untended would have accomplished.

The wetland is still a work in progress. Permits have been filed, design crews engaged. We birders are staying vigilant, ensuring that the project doesn't get forgotten amid the agendas of industrial expansion. We are under no illusions that this is a solution. Even as we are working to enhance this one wetland, the Port is expanding its reach to the south, taking over farmlands and forests for more industry. Maybe an electric car maker will build there, they said in their board meeting, trying to appeal to the group of environmentalists present. But we know that industry is industry, and as long as it marches forward, there will still be devastation and loss, whatever is being built.

To plant a garden, to create a wetland—these seem like small acts in the face of our world of concrete, our obsession with never-ending economic growth. What difference can it make? I think of G. K. Chesterton's comment, in his wonderful economic critique, *The Outline of Sanity*, which takes aim at industrial capitalism's takeover of small shops and farms:

> *Do anything, however small, that will prevent the completion of the work of capitalist combination. Do anything that will even delay that completion. Save one shop out of a hundred shops. . . . Keep open one door out of a hundred doors; for so long as one door is open, we are not in prison. Ahab has not his kingdom so long as Naboth has his vineyard. Haman will not be happy in the palace while Mordecai is sitting in the gate. A hundred tales of human history are there to show that*

> *tendencies can be turned back, and that one stumbling-block can be the turning point. The sands of time are simply dotted with single stakes that have thus marked the turn of the tide.*

In Chesterton's stirring words, we find a purpose for our hospitality. By turning our yard toward reconciliation and welcome for wild creatures, we are keeping open the possibility of a different future. If my yard can host an increasing variety of life, linked with other yards doing the same, then we are joining together in an act of resistance rather than capitulating to the aesthetics of the golf course.

Hospitality is more than resistance, however; it is also a sacramental practice—a way by which we learn to recognize the holy in the wild lives around us. "There are no unsacred places," writes Wendell Berry, "there are only sacred places and desecrated places." The practice of reconciliation ecology is an act in which we relate to the world in its sacredness, keeping ourselves from seeing it as a mere landscape or an interchangeable abstraction for our desires.

I think here of the Orthodox churches of Ethiopia, many of which preserve a belt of forest around their buildings to resemble a renewed Eden. Those sacred forests are now providing the seeds for restoration in the larger landscape, which has been decimated by extractive agriculture. What if we kept alive our yards, the marginal places in the midst of our cities, our places of worship and work, as sacred—not only as places of hospitality for the wild now but also as sources of hospitality for the future? What if each yard could host the future of the planet by holding onto the life needed to reseed the world when we finally wake from the delusions of our extractive ways of life? It's a possibility I hope for through my small acts of hospitality in the place to which I belong.

After I had glimpsed the harrier, my hundredth yard-bird, the backhoe operator did his work. Despite his great care to preserve our trees, there was a scar of mud and shale—the substrate of most ground in this place—running along the side of my yard. I went to the website of a company that grows native seeds for my region and ordered a mix recommended for erosion control. Covering the ground with straw, I spread the seeds of tickseed, bluestem, ironweed, and over twenty other native plants that would take hold in this disturbed soil.

Perhaps from this scar an even better ecosystem could come. Perhaps, eventually, by raking these seeds into the ground, I will beckon new species to share this place with me and all those who call this ground home.

4

APRIL

Abundance

WE STOPPED FOR lunch in the aptly named Pineland, Texas, at a place called "Jimmy's Home Cooking." It was a portable building next to a rundown snow-cone trailer where a baby rocked, unattended, under a canopy of blue tarps, and an assortment of what seemed to be Jimmy's family and friends lounged around, seemingly unoccupied on this particular Monday. The menu for Jimmy's was written on a dry-erase board, where half the items were smudged off. Home cooking, it seemed, was mostly accomplished through the combined powers of a can opener, a freezer, and a deep fryer. I decided, given that we were in Texas, I should go for the brisket.

While we waited for the food, Evan and I checked the latest bird sightings in the area. It turned out we were close to the Angeline National Forest, where Red-cockaded Woodpeckers and Bachman's Sparrows nest. We'd made good time through the morning, having left Arkansas shortly after dawn, so we decided it would be worth a detour of an hour or so before we made our way to the coast.

Evan and I are both Episcopal priests. Having just celebrated the high days of Holy Week culminating with Easter, we'd taken a week off to bird the upper Texas coast around Galveston and High Island. It was mid-April, right around my birthday, and if all went well, we'd witness one of the most intense birding areas of the entire country close to its peak season.

With a surprisingly decent plate of brisket in hand, we decided to pay a visit to Sam Rayburn Lake in search of the sparrows and woodpeckers. The area around the lake is an example of what good forest management can do. The pine forest here wasn't the thick, uniform woods of a pine plantation—trees grown in the style of mono-crop agriculture to be pulped into fiber for Amazon shipping boxes. Instead, this pine forest was open, with large trees interspersed with a herbaceous understory of sedges and flowering plants like Texas bullnettle, blooming with large white flowers. The mature pines were charred in places, evidence of the controlled burns that are used to manage this forest, burns that reflect the ecology in which these pines are most at home.

Across the street, on private land, the forest was choked with privet and other invasive understory plants. These forests were never burned, and it was clear that the ecology was different. We heard towhees and cardinals—common birds that favor the habitats of human landscapes—but there was no possibility for the unique species that we hoped to find in the mature pine forest. There would be no Red-cockaded Woodpecker or Bachman's Sparrow on the privet side, so we kept our scan toward the left of the road, looking for the running pine sap that would tell us Red-cockaded Woodpeckers had been there.

Red-cockaded Woodpeckers are among the most endangered birds in North America. No nesting site is left unmonitored, and we soon learned to look for painted white bands on the trees that indicated nest cavities that had been active in recent years. With black-and-white checkered backs, the Red-cockaded resembles the common Downy Woodpecker. Unlike the Downy, however, these birds create nesting cavities in living pine trees. Their cavities are evident from the sap that runs down the tree's sides wherever the nest hole has been excavated.

The woodpeckers will only nest in mature pine trees, and they favor forests in which those pines are widely spaced. This was once a winning strategy, before the days of widespread fire suppression and logging. But with the coming of European colonialists to the southern forests, their numbers began to diminish. Thankfully, the Red-cockaded Woodpeckers' plight was recognized before it was too late. Unlike the Ivory-billed Woodpecker and the Bachman's Warbler, both species who went extinct because of habitat loss, the Red-cockaded Woodpecker was lucky enough to have humans put effort into preserving nesting colonies. This forest was one example of the kind of management that is helping this unique species hold on.

That some species would require such specific habitats might seem like a flaw in the systems of nature. Instead, it reflects the abundance of life, a joyful mix that fills every corner and every place. The tragedy of modern life is not our abundance of variety but our depletion of it. We think that, because we can order anything from Amazon, listen to more music than we can imagine on Spotify, and watch more films than our ancestors would have thought possible on Netflix, we are living in a time of abundance. But the truth is that our experiences, the varieties of life in which we engage, are ever more uniform. "A hundred channels and nothing on," has become a basic fact of life.

Birding, however, leads us into a different possibility—an opening to the joys of true abundance. The world of life has been forming to the contours of variety for millennia, with every niche filled, down to the microbiomes of insects.

To be a birder is to become a connoisseur of habitats. There are even field guides dedicated to habitats, illustrating and outlining their major forms. But no book could contain the variety of homemaking that creatures perform throughout the world. The more unique this homemaking is, the less competition a species has. And yet, in cases like the Red-cockaded Woodpecker, this uniqueness can also become a liability. One's unique way of life can become threatened by the monocultures of modernity.

We followed the road around a bend, the pavement turning to gravel. Here, both sides of the road were open pine forest, and just as we came to a power-line cut, we heard a singing sparrow. It was an unfamiliar song to me. Though I am by no means perfect in my recall, when you have birded for long enough in the Eastern forests, an unfamiliar song usually means something good. "I think that's a Bachman's Sparrow!" I exclaimed as Evan pulled the car to the shoulder.

These elusive sparrows are hard to find, except for in spring, when they sing readily in the early hours of the morning. It was now well into the afternoon, so we were lucky that this bird, amped up on breeding-season hormones, was keeping the morning song going. We found the Bachman's Sparrow on a high perch, but when it saw us it dropped to the ground, where it knew it could hide more easily. Drab and striped with varied shades of brown, it sported camouflage perfectly suited for the habitat. Still, it continued to sing, and the two of us worked together to use an impromptu trigonometry to find its location so that we could see it again.

Soon we spotted the bird on a low shrub, from where it hopped to the ground and ran along a fallen log. Finally we were able to get good looks at this elusive sparrow, one I hadn't seen in a decade or more, and an altogether new bird for Evan. One of the joys of birding is sharing in the new, and this trip had the potential to bring Evan a host of "life birds": species a person encounters for the first time in life. I was hoping for a few "lifers" myself.

We continued our drive, skirting lakeside houses here and there and turning again into the pine woods. Our windows were down, and we strained against the sound of crunching gravel to hear the sound of woodpeckers.

We were guided in our search by red dots on the map of our birding apps, images that allowed us to know exactly where others had reported the woodpeckers in recent days. Though I tend to be a Luddite, or at least wish I could be, GPS and cell phones have revolutionized birding. Many serious birders keep public and nearly instantaneous lists of the birds they've seen through eBird. This makes it far easier than in the past to get real-time updates on where a bird was last spotted.

We drove toward one of those dots, and soon saw the white bands painted on the pine trees. Several of the bands looked fresh, which indicated researchers were actively monitoring nest sites. Looking up, we saw sap pooling out from around the nest holes, resembling candle wax running down a Chianti bottle in an Italian restaurant.

Then, high in a tree, we spotted a woodpecker. Sure enough, it was a female Red-cockaded, her body a checkered patchwork of black and white with a bright white cheek. She flew from the treetop to the nesting cavity, giving us a clear view. Soon she was joined by another bird, a male, probably her mate. In time we saw two other pairs, the woodpeckers hopping around the pines, preening, calling, doing woodpecker things. Seeing these endangered birds, carrying on life and holding hope for the future, was a moment of intense joy.

The medieval theologian St. Thomas Aquinas wrote that true joy comes when we are in the presence of one we love or when we see the good of that love accomplished. When we love someone, even when we are apart from them, we rejoice when some good comes their way, and we lament when some ill happens to them. Thomas, as he's known in philosophical circles, was speaking of love for other humans, but I think the same could be said for birds.

Watching birds, wondering at their beauty, and learning about their lives all cultivate a love for these creatures. And with that love, we are invited into joy when we are in their presence. So it's a double joy when we see their good fulfilled. Evan and I felt joy watching those woodpeckers, which had no idea of their endangered lives. Here, at least, they were safe, and a new generation would soon emerge from those sap-oozing holes. It was affection that made their lives possible—the love of many who had decided that they would dedicate time, effort, and money to ensure that these creatures are not counted on the all-too-long list of the extinct. We who simply get to watch and benefit from such good work can at least let our hearts leap, can at least have joy at these unique lives kept with wild care for the moment.

The first full morning of birding, we visited a bayside marsh at the far western end of Galveston Island. It was just past the condo where we were staying, which was owned by the sister of one of Evan's friends. This place didn't show up on any hotspot maps, but Evan had been there on a previous trip and promised it would be a good beginning.

As we drove into the area, we were met by blackberry bushes heavy with fruit. The thorny vines grew in lush clusters, bordering concrete pads with the studs of old electrical conduit and plumbing sticking out here and there. A hurricane had wiped out what had once been a neighborhood. Never rebuilt, it was being reclaimed by the wild.

In her book *Believers: Making a Life at the End of the World*, Lisa Wells introduces the word *ruderal* to name a hope she has for this moment. Drawn from the Latin word for rubble, ruderal describes plants that, as *Webster's* describes it, are "growing where the natural vegetational cover has been disturbed by humans." "I've become attached to this term 'ruderal,'" writes Wells, "and to the idea of a ruderal legacy." She goes on to write that these ruderal plants offer her the hope that "ways of life are possible in which human beings not only thrive but also repair damage and even *increase* the biodiversity and beauty of the planet."

Blackberries are a ruderal plant par excellence. They do not require good soil but instead protect the ground. With their fruit they attract birds and animals, all of them carrying seeds on their bodies and in their manure. Through that manure, the ground becomes host for more life, plants sprouting in the shelter of the vines. From that nursery of thorns, trees sprout and grow, and with them the diversity of the place compounds, each succession of life increasing in diversity until it becomes a settled home, a symbiotic whole of shared and varied life.

Unlike so many aspects of ecological life where I feel like an outsider to the wild banquet, blackberries ripe with fruit are an invitation for me to become a participant in the landscape, a diner at the ruderal feast. Perhaps it is some trace of my evolutionary past, or my childhood of picking blackberries wherever I found them, but I have a sense of abundance whenever I am in the presence of fruiting blackberry vines. And though I've grown the thornless varieties, cultivated for agriculture, no berries are better than the wild ones that require scratched hands and chigger bites to gather.

The old concrete road led around a bend, descending slightly toward the bay's edge before disappearing into a cracked and muddy mess. We parked where the pavement ended, gathered our scopes, and moved toward the water. This was a place of many edges, with niche habitats intersecting like pieces of fabric on a quilt of life. There were low saltwater grasses and sedges, tall reeds, shrubby dryland plants, the muddy edges of marsh pools, and the sandy shore of the bay itself. In each place, birds were making a life, each enjoying its place in the patchwork.

The soundscape was dominated by Great-tailed Grackles. The males, amped on the testosterone flush of breeding season, were loud and showy, throwing their heads back, puffing out their chests, and letting out their metallic songs. Toward the bay, the sound of Laughing Gulls joined the raucous choir, with terns and skimmers and a dozen lesser voices adding their notes.

On the sandy beach, there were large clusters of birds, arranged in mixed bands of black and gray and white. The Black Skimmers were the largest; a coastal specialty, these birds feed exclusively from the water. They glide along low and close to the surface, especially at dawn and dusk and even into the night, running the bottom half of their huge bills through the water. When they hit a fish, their bills snap shut automatically, quickly catching the fish like a mouse in a trap.

Beside them, in a cluster of their own, were Royal Terns. These are the punk rock birds of the coast, sporting bold black caps that crest into spikes at the back of their heads. Their loud calls, raspy and pitched, fit their vibe. Beside them were the smaller Forster's Terns, slender and elegant with folded wings, with a few closely related Common Terns scattered among the group. To round out the mix was a group of Sandwich Terns, some in a beautiful, faintly rose-hued breeding plumage that is hard to do justice to in a photo.

All this diversity is a product of abundance in finitude, the pattern in nature by which one species changes over time to fill the many niches of a place. It was the observation of this diversity among the finches of the Galapagos Islands that led the young Charles Darwin to begin his wonderings that would eventually become the theory of evolution by natural selection. Often framed in terms of competition and survival of the fittest, Darwin's insight is just as much a recognition of how diversity creates abundance. And that abundance, in turn, creates within us a sense of joy, of well-being. What delight would we feel if there was only one finch adapted to one ecosystem?

Documentary filmmaker Craig Foster, who became well known for his film *My Octopus Teacher*, described in an interview the profound sense of psychological distress that can come when we are not surrounded by diverse forms of life: "If you are in an environment where there's almost no biodiversity, your ancient creature that's living inside you, your deep design, is terrified because it doesn't know you can go to the supermarket. It's just looking and feeling and hearing and smelling—there's no life around." Going to wild places, spaces full of diverse life, however, can give us a sense of fullness and well-being, a sense of joy. As Foster explains it, "going to these wilderness places tells that wild part of us that everything is okay, that . . . there's plenty for everybody and we just need to go and harvest a tiny bit each day and there'll be plenty for everybody, for the family. And you feel, oh, everything's all right, everything will be fine. This is good. This is the good life."

Just being in the presence of such a variety of life gives a sense of wholeness that reaches deep into who we are as humans. But I think there is also more than a merely naturalistic explanation for all of this. We are a part of a larger whole of life, and when we allow ourselves to wonder and marvel at it, we are given the great gift of participation rather than proprietorship. It is a pity that so many of us can identify more brands of consumer products than we can wild things; that our only sense of diversity and abundance is all the things available to us in a supermarket or the long list of products that can be ordered online. Joy comes with welcoming the life of which we are merely members rather owners and managers.

In fact, the joy of abundant life takes us to the very question of what it means to be a human being. In an essay on this theme, the Eastern Orthodox theologian and bishop John Zizioulas offers two competing possibilities for the human role in creation—proprietors or priests. Proprietorship is simple enough to understand. It is likely the dominant view, especially in those places formed by the capitalist conception of the world. We are the owners of the world, ready to make it serve our purposes. We may give thanks to God for the gift of the world, but we do not accept that God has already called this gift good, that we can simply savor and enjoy it. We live in the legacy of the Enlightenment philosopher John Locke, who said that the gifts of God were simply raw material without any intrinsic value. Such "gifts," according to Locke, can only be made good and useful through our labor. For Locke, land and animals, trees and streams are not valuable in themselves but only when human work turns them into a product or resource. Under the spell of this view, we have lost a sense of the world's grace and the inherent goodness of the Creation.

To be a priest, however, is to be one who blesses: one who names the holy in the world and calls creation toward the great end for which it was made. For a priest, the world is determined by worship, not some worth established through an economy. Zizioulas believes that the unique role that human beings have in the order of all creation is to call the world to join in this blessedness. "The priest is the one who freely takes the world in his hands to refer it to God, and who, in return, brings God's blessing to what he refers to God," writes Zizioulas.

We saw nearly forty species of birds during our time at this marsh made in the ruins of a neighborhood, ranging from the terns on the beaches to Wilson's Plovers on the mudflats to Seaside Sparrows hiding among the grasses. But we saw perhaps the strangest bird toward the end of our time. As we traipsed back toward Evan's car through the brackish marsh, a bird barely larger than a football flushed from the reeds and flew into a cluster of cattails. It held itself aloft, balanced between two stalks, the upper part of its body seeming to be all neck, with two white eyes and dark stripes on either side. It was colorful in a camouflaged way, with a faded red wash on its wings and rusty orange extending up the sides of its neck. This was a Least Bittern, an annual resident in these coastal marshes and a summer resident across much of the Eastern United States. Though not rare in the right habitat, bitterns aren't your run-of-the-mill birds, and it had been many years since I'd seen one.

This bittern, one of the smallest members of the heron family, stood between the stalks and looked at us with what seemed to be a kind of curiosity. Though we shared the same world, our lifeways were as alien to one another as if we had come from different planets. We looked at the bird and the bird looked at us, both curious about the other.

Most birders experience this at some point or another: when the watcher discovers they are also the watched. I have often walked a trail, only to look up and see a bird leaning over to get a better look at me. But the most magical moment, the one with the greatest joy, is when there is an encounter—not just a looking at each other, but a kind of mutual recognition. That is what I sensed in this bittern as he looked at us, perched between the cattail stalks.

After the moment had passed, he dropped down and disappeared into the dense cluster of vegetation. We left, elated. The trip had barely begun, and already we were immersed in abundance.

The hard thing about a birding trip is that between the refuges, traveling from marsh to shore to remnant woodland, you come to understand what has been lost. Each tract of housing, each convenience store and beachfront megastore stocked full of next week's shoreline trash has taken the place of a marsh, or scrub oak forest, or field of grass and sedge. As joyful as abundance can be, birders know abundance by its negative as well. *Biopaucity* is a term to describe a world poor in life. It is, in many ways, our world. The challenge is that the world is also so rich with life that it is hard to see when it has been diminished. We are like third-generation Vanderbilts, living in gilded mansions, enjoying lives that are still luxurious even if the bank accounts are running out and our estates will soon be resort hotels.

Driving east along the shores of Galveston Island, I try to imagine the long history here. This was an early colonial settlement, and before that, a foraging place for varied tribes and nations of Indigenous people who would come to collect oysters and fish from the abundance of the Gulf. Was there a fishing village where the Denny's now stands?

The history of human presence, especially of colonialist and capitalist life, is one of extraction. Galveston stands by the center of the most menacing of those forms—the vast network of oil rigs off the coast and refineries across the bay. Oil represents both the abundance of the earth, its tremendous stored energy, and the terrors of extraction and loss. The great wealth—the full life that was made possible through oil—came at the detriment of that wider and varied abundance that is planetary life. We have traded the abundance of diversity and variety for the singular abundance of one thing: numbers on a balance sheet. It is proving not only dissatisfying but destructive.

Galveston was once home to a unique, ground-dwelling bird with a striped back and bright yellow bulges of skin on the throat of males. These skin pouches would balloon during elaborate courtship displays that would rival any of those put on by the famed Birds of Paradise. Named Attwater's Prairie Chicken, these birds once lived in abundance in coastal grasslands—places kept free of trees by a mix of fires and hurricanes. But a mix of invasive plants, fire suppression, and development led to such a steep decline in their populations that they were soon classified as endangered.

A subspecies of the Greater Prairie Chicken, a group of Attwater's Prairie Chickens lived and bred in an area set aside by the Nature Conservancy just across the bay from Galveston. But in 1999 the Nature Conservancy allowed oil drilling on the site. As a result, Attwater's Prairie Chickens have now completely disappeared from the area. It is unlikely that this unique subspecies of bird will survive, and its prairie chicken relatives are also threatened throughout their range.

True abundance, the sort that is represented by diverse life, cannot be had by money or the compromises used to get it. From an ecological point of view, abundance is a product of frugality—all using only what they need and leaving the extra for others. To live in a world of true abundance, we need not sell off good habitat to benefit from the money made from oil wells, as the Nature Conservancy did. Instead, we should learn to live in a smaller, simpler way so that fewer such wells will be required. Like hospitality, abundance is made possible by making room. True abundance requires participation rather than possession.

The writer L. M. Sacasas introduced me to the idea of holding onto certain phrases or quotes as a kind of amulet, words imbued with power. As Sacasas describes it, "Like an amulet worn around the neck, these words might somehow shield or guide or console or sustain the one who held them close to mind and heart." When thinking about the room needed for our common abundance, there are two such amulets I hold close.

The first is a condensation of a quote from Gandhi, widely known as "we have enough for everyone's need, but not for everyone's greed." In the speech from which that pithy version was derived, Gandhi said, "I suggest that we are thieves in a way. If I take anything that I do not need for my own immediate use and keep it, I thieve it from somebody else. I venture to suggest that it is the fundamental law of Nature, without exception, that Nature produces enough for our wants from day to day, and if only everybody took enough for himself and nothing more, there would be no pauperism in this world, there would be no more dying of starvation in this world. But so long as we have got this inequality, so long we are thieving."

The other, which echoes Gandhi, comes from Wendell Berry. It is a quote I've posted on my bulletin board, one I read again and again as a continual challenge: "The religion and the environmentalism of the highly industrialized countries are at bottom a sham, because they make it their business to fight against something that they do not really wish to destroy. We all live by robbing nature, but our standard of living demands that the robbery shall continue. We must achieve the character and acquire the skills to live much poorer than we do."

In both these amulets I sense not a condemnation but a call—I am reminded of what is at stake in my gluttonous hunger, always wanting more. And yet, if I stop and learn to wait in the abundance of what is here, then my desires turn. I want the more that is already here—far more than I want a life of more square feet or a fancier vehicle or shoes for every occasion. When those hungers arise, I try to remember that by limiting my wants for such things, I am offering life to others. True abundance is always shared abundance, and nothing is more joyful.

Over the days that followed, there was no hint of a world impoverished. We stood on Bolivar Flats and watched a flock of America Avocets that numbered in the thousands, all turning toward the peach colors of their breeding plumage. Along a marshy road we heard the strange metallic songs of Nelson's Sparrows. And at Anahuac National Wildlife Refuge, we followed an auto loop through open swamp lands, where Common Gallinules waded alongside dozens of alligators, many well over eight feet long, lazy in the afternoon sun.

Everywhere there were birds and with them birders. I was glad to be with Evan as he got this first taste of the wider world of bird-watchers. Though I love my solitary ventures into the wild world, joining with so many others who share this common love brings its own unique joy. And with the peak of spring migration lasting only a few weeks, we had come at the beginning of a time when people from across the world were, like the birds themselves, funneling through this one area of Texas.

On one afternoon, we traveled to Smith Oaks. When I think of birding the Texas Gulf Coast, this small patch of woodlands, along with Bolivar Flats, Sabine Woods, Boy Scout Woods, and Anahuac, are what come to mind. My first time here was in my early teens, when my father was invited to speak at a camp in East Texas in mid-April. My birthday was then, and since we were already traveling far, we decided to make a vacation of it. It was my birthday week, just as this week was, and I said a trip to High Island was what I wanted.

I urged my parents to make a hotel reservation far ahead of time, but they didn't sense any urgency. They simply could not imagine that there were so many people who shared their son's strange hobby and that no hotels would be available for miles. As we neared High Island, however, it became clear there was no room in any inn, hotel, motel, or bed and breakfast within miles of High Island. We had to drive over an hour from the primary hotspots to finally find a place with vacancies. It was, to this day, the worst hotel I've ever stayed in, with crumbs in the sheets and roaches scuttling around the room at night.

My father woke with me early, in the pre-dawn, and we drove back to the town of High Island where we stopped for breakfast in one of the handful of cafés. It was bustling with birders, everyone with binoculars around their necks or propped beside their plates. At the restaurant's entrance, alongside the menu, was a dry-erase board with a list of interesting sightings in the area.

It was a thrill to hear people with so many accents, both from across America and the world, who had come to witness the abundance that could be found in a small patch of woods in April. I felt like I had found my people. That morning I witnessed trees laden with warblers, thrushes hopping everywhere along the path, and tanagers flashing their bold reds from the canopy. It was, or was very nearly, a "fallout"—a time when birds that have struggled through rough winds and rain over the Gulf land in the first decent habitat they can find. A fallout is a perilous time for birds. But for birders, it is an experience of wonder. Birds with clear skies and a good tail wind might continue flying for miles after reaching land, but when they are forced down all at once in a fallout, birders experience a concentration of birds found in few other places.

I returned to High Island in my late teens, this time as part of a team of young birders (we called ourselves the Thrashers) competing in the Great Texas Birding Classic—a series of three "big day" competitions along three sections of the Texas coast. The first of these was on the upper coast, of which High Island is a part. We had one of the highest big-day totals recorded for Texas at the time, with nearly two hundred species in a single day, a major accomplishment for a group of gangly teenaged birders.

Now I was returning after decades away, and the sense of joy stirred again as we drove the road through the low, brushy woods leading to Smith Oaks. Smith Oaks and Boy Scout Woods are the most famous of four preserves in High Island owned by the Houston Audubon Society. The town itself is unincorporated, with around five hundred people living in its handful of neighborhoods. It is not, properly, an island in the land-surrounded-on-all-sides-by-water sense. The name comes, instead, from its unique elevation—a rise of around thirty-eight feet above sea level formed by a salt dome beneath the ground. The formation makes High Island the highest point of land on the Gulf Coast between Mobile, Alabama, and the Yucatan Peninsula.

At Smith Oaks, we pulled into the parking lot and made our way to the tent where we paid the small admission fee that helps support the preserves. It was mid-afternoon, the best time to bird this area, since it is around that time that many migrants arrive after their trans-Gulf flights. We walked past the remains of an old schoolhouse and toward the first of the preserve's drips.

Birds are attracted to moving water, so at sanctuaries like this bird baths with a dripping pipe are used to lure birds from the deeper woods. At the nearby Boy Scout Woods, there are even stadium seats around their main drip pool, a place where dozens of birders can gather to watch as warblers, thrushes, tanagers, and other migrants come in for a drink or bath.

At this drip, a tour group was gathered, watching as a yellow-breasted bird with an olive back and black face mask hopped around the pool of water. It was a Kentucky Warbler, a species I'd helped to study as a teenager. Though it is named for the state in which early ornithologists first collected specimens of the bird, most of the breeding population of Kentucky Warblers actually nest in Arkansas. Seeing one always feels like encountering an old friend, and here on the Texas coast, it felt to me like a chance encounter in an airport. Both of us were far away from home, on our way from here to there.

After adding several species to our checklists at the drip, we continued along the path toward some raucous noise at the refuge center. Smith Oaks hosts a rookery, a strange phenomenon of mostly water-loving birds that nest in the bird equivalent of a big city high-rise apartment. On an island that protects the rookery from predators like raccoons and coyotes, an array of egrets, herons, spoonbills, anhingas, and cormorants all had nests piled on branches up and down the trees. Many of these birds are silent when encountered in the field, but here in the rookery they were loudly calling, each dialing up the volume to be heard over the other. On the shore of the island, huge alligators waited, ready to snatch up any unfortunate baby bird that fell from the nest.

We continued around the pond, watching for movement in the trees, ready to spot the hints of a warbler above. Others were doing the same, and when one person's binoculars went up, others' followed suit. At an intersection of two paths, a young woman was looking though her lenses at the branches above. She had a warbler, she said, but it had disappeared before she'd been able to identify it. Beautiful and lively, warblers are among the most sought-after and frustrating birds. "Warbler neck" is a unique ailment among birders who spend the spring with their faces turned upward, trying to spot these wonders as they hop high among the branches.

Another birder came up, reporting that a Cerulean Warbler had been seen just down the path. This is a scarce bird, one I encounter once or twice per season if I'm lucky. Preferring large, unbroken deciduous forests for its nesting, the Cerulean Warbler has not fared well in the age of deforestation, roads, and power-line cuts. A gem among gems, with its blue back, white chest, and dark black streaks down the side, these are among the most beautiful warblers, a bird that is easy to love.

Even nonbirders may recognize the Cerulean Warbler from the novelist Jonathan Franzen's best-selling tragicomic novel *Freedom*. The bird appears on the cover and is a central part of the plot, with one of its main characters, Walter Berglund, dedicating his life to creating a preserve for the bird. In order to achieve the preserve, Berglund decides to compromise: Let West Virginia coal companies extract all they can from the land before setting up a vast area as a permanent forest preserve. It's a classic Faustian bargain, and it goes as most do. Walter is only successful in opening lands for coal mining, not in creating the habitat he'd hoped for. Franzen is among our sharpest moral voices, a serious birder himself, and he knows all too well the dangers of such compromises.

We want it both ways: to achieve an abundance both ecological and economic. But such achievements will never come to be. We must decide: the abundance of the living systems of the earth for millennia, or the abundance of money for a little while. It seems an obvious choice, but we continue—I continue—to struggle making it.

We followed the path around Smith Pond, and as we did, the birds seemed to become more active. Instead of a warbler here or there, suddenly birds began appearing everywhere, our pace slowing as we tried to catch sight of the birds. In one tree, a Black-billed Cuckoo appeared, a western cousin of the Yellow-billed Cuckoo that is ubiquitous in the Arkansas woods in summer. A fairly uncommon bird, it was a good find and was cooperative enough to give us good looks at its distinctive red eye and eponymous black bill.

We seemed to have arrived right at the high point of oriole migration, with both Baltimore and Orchard Orioles gathering in a mulberry tree laden with fruit. Soon the orioles—orange, rust, and yellow—were joined by Rose-breasted Grosbeaks, the males with their jet-black backs, white bellies, and crimson-splashed chests, the females resembling large sparrows with streaks of brown. Several other birders joined us as the fruit-eating frenzy gathered more and more birds, seemingly appearing from nowhere. The accents of exclamation around us were British, American, and Quebecois French, all uttering amazed commands to "look!" at their companions.

We left, eventually, full from the feast. On our way back to the car, a Swainson's Hawk teetered overhead, and both Louisiana and Northern Waterthrushes bobbed on the marshy edge of the lake. Our senses were saturated with the abundance, our eyes and ears exhausted from all the looking and listening, but our hearts full of the joy of it all.

The thing about abundance is that it is hard to contain. I could write a whole book recounting all we saw in those five days. But eventually we had to go home. A few days after our return, I rode my bike along the Arkansas River with my binoculars slung to my side. Pelicans were still gathered on the sand bars, and a few cormorants flew by. Already these species were dwindling in numbers as they left their winter in the south for their summer homes to the north. Then, from a riverside sycamore, I heard the chatter of a Baltimore Oriole. I looked into the leaves and there a small group of the birds were moving among the branches, the males with their classic orange and black, the females in their yellow and black.

Were those some of the same orioles I'd seen over four hundred miles away in Texas a few days before? It is possible. To imagine that possibility is a kind of recognition of the grand dance that is migration, a window into the vast wonder and abundance of the world.

5

MAY

Listening

THE TIME WAS 4 a.m. on the western edge of Little Rock. We stood outside the car, pulled off the road in the driveway of a prep-school baseball field, with our hands cupped behind our ears. Across the blacktop was a patch of woods, bisected by a power-line cut, flanked on either side by neighborhoods that encroach on its borders each year. For three years running, this has been the home of an Eastern Screech Owl, a small tree-dwelling bird that calls with an eerie whinny and low trill.

I had in my hand a small Bluetooth speaker, from which I played a recording of the owl. I can sometimes whistle well enough to get one to respond, but I wanted to take no chances on how convincing I could sound. We needed to find this bird to add to our list. This was the beginning of the annual BirdAR Big Day competition—a time each spring when teams of birders go out to see who can tally the most species in Arkansas in a single twenty-four-hour period. Any wild and free bird, heard or seen by at least two team members, could count for our list. I'm competitive by nature, and I hoped that this year we could break our record. To do so, we'd need as many nocturnal birds as possible to begin our list.

The speaker blasted the sound of the owl through a few rounds of calls. Then I hit stop and we again cupped our ears to listen. A car passed, somewhere in the distance a dog barked, and very far in the distance we could hear a Chuck-wills-widow, a bird we gladly logged on our list. But we heard no Screech Owls.

Since last spring, when we had heard two Screech Owls at this same spot, a large silver box had appeared. It emitted a low hum that made it difficult for us to hear anything in the direction of the woods. The neighborhoods were also closer. A new development had begun to the east of the patch of the forest, and some of the woods had been cleared to make way. We could now see the lights of houses through the narrowing strip of trees. The Screech Owls, it seems, had moved on.

When looking for owls, or rather listening for them, I go in order of predation. Screech Owls are a meal for a Great Horned Owl, so beginning by playing this large predator's call would discourage the smaller birds from revealing their location. With the Screech Owls quiet, however, I turned to playing the hoots of the Great Horned Owl. Almost immediately we saw one. Perhaps it had already come close because of the Screech Owl calls, but as soon as we played its low hoots, a bird flew to the top of one the power-line poles. In the glow of the neighborhood streetlights, we could see the horned silhouette. Soon it was joined by another bird, meaning this was a pair, who had probably already established this area as their territory, perhaps with a nest nearby. Great Horned Owls nest early, sometimes beginning even in February. By early May, they likely already had fledglings.

The owls flew, just a few yards from us, in complete silence. At the leading edge of their wings, owls have comb-like serrations that break the air as it passes over their wings, dampening the sound. Their feathers are also covered with a soft, velvety material that helps muffle wind passing over it. These adaptations are important for owls because most of their prey—small rodents like mice and voles—rely on extremely good hearing to protect them from predators. In a game of adaptive one-upmanship, the owls had become like the stealth fighter planes of the bird world—undetectable by even the most sensitive ears.

We watched for a moment as the two owls sat, looking down on us, before they both, on some hidden signal, disappeared silently into the woods. We had two nocturnal birds for the day, and dawn would come soon; we had to keep moving.

Our team had formed from our usual Christmas Bird Count group. We worked well together, and given that we enjoyed a day of birding in the cold of December, we thought a spring day at the height of migration would be even better. With David being an engineer, and Ari a science journalist, and me a priest, ready to pray for the hidden to become visible, we also had a good mix of skills. A birding day like this is a test not only of the ability to identify birds but also how to plan a good route that will allow both maximizing species while minimizing dead time.

Birding is often called "birdwatching," but the truth of the matter is that many more birds can be *heard* than *watched*. Especially at times like spring and summer, when bird vocalizations are at their peak, far more birds can be found by listening than by seeing. Birds are beautiful, and even the most dully colored are a wonder to watch, but many birds use hiding from the eyes of potential predators as one of their key strategies of survival. Even when they may be visible, our eyesight usually needs the aid of binoculars or spotting scopes to see them. Yet for all their hiding, birds call and sing constantly and loudly, communicating with one another about their whereabouts and the happenings of the forest community around them. A birder who has trained their ears to listen and to understand these bird calls can not only identify more species but can also be clued into what is happening in the forest—from the approach of another person to the arrival of an aerial predator.

On a Big Day competition, listening is critical. Our goal was to identify well over 130 species for the day. Such a total couldn't come without having a large number of those birds as "heard only." And the truth is that for many types of birds, the only way to ultimately identify them is by call. Learning to listen, then, is an essential practice in a birder's life.

Our perceptions tend toward the visual. We look, watch, read—all with our eyes. Increasingly, even audiovisual content is presented with closed captioning for those who have no hearing loss. Many of us spend our days looking at screens, we use text messages more than phone calls to communicate, and we scroll through social media posts that feature videos with the audio automatically turned off. When we do listen, it is often to music as a background, something to drown out the general noise of our machine world.

Because the modern world is so noisy, it feels easier to just use our eyes rather than to really listen to the world around us. Writing now, at my dining room table, I can hear the washing machine churning, the refrigerator humming, and some unidentified high-pitched machine sound coming from outside. These kinds of sounds have become the regular backdrop of life, and so we understandably want to just tune them out. But in doing so, we are missing the songs and sounds of the world itself. We can catch them only if we learn again to listen and, in turn, to hear.

Learning to listen puts us in touch with the particulars of a place. Each place has its unique sounds, the individuated mix of the local chorus. Blindfold a good birder and take them to a forest and they could tell you, in broad strokes, what kind of landscape they are in, the trees and shrubs present. If there are Golden-crowned Kinglets in abundance, there are pines about. A large flock of Goldfinches in winter means gum trees. The high-pitched whistles of Cedar Waxwings say that there are berries to be had.

Birding provides an opening toward listening, a habit that provides the skills for everything from hearing good music to paying attention to a conversation. By tuning ourselves carefully to birds, an awareness is opened for all the other times when such focused attention is required. Through years of intense listening to birds, I am immediately aware of their calls around me, whether I am actively "birding" or not.

Sitting outside at a family gathering, amid a picnic conversation, I might hear a Pine Warbler overhead, a Summer Tanager from the edge of a lake, a Yellow-throated Warbler high in an oak, or a Red-headed Woodpecker rattling from a snag. These songs and calls come into my awareness without any conscious action.

In Italo Calvino's novel *If On a Winter's Night a Traveler*, there is a character who has learned how not to read. He makes sculptures of the books that no longer have meaning for him other than as pure objects. *Unlearning* something is an intriguing idea, because once we have unlocked a form of perception, it is hard to turn it off. Try *not* to read when you see a text or a newspaper article or a book cover, and you'll see just how hard it is. And that automatic listening to the birds around me is how more than thirty years of birding has changed my hearing. I can't help but listen and seek to know the birds I hear.

In many ways, this kind of listening awareness is like the work of prayer. In its deepest forms, prayer is about hearing God, and deliberate time set aside for this task is where we begin to hear the songs and calls of the divine voice.

You learn bird calls, in the oldest and best way, by hearing something unfamiliar and then following the sound until you find the bird. At times it could turn out to be a familiar bird offering an unfamiliar sound; at others, it could be an unknown bird, a rarity or a species whose songs you've never learned. Learning to hear God is like this, too: We hear various noises in the silence and follow them where they lead. Sometimes it is the siren of some misplaced desire we hear. But at times we find some new reality of the divine singing in our hearts.

It is through the deliberate and focused periods of prayer that we learn to hear the voice that then continues to sound in all the moments of our days. There are few places where I do not hear birds. It is a sound we often tune out or cover over. But when you've trained your attention to hear it, you will notice the songs everywhere.

From the suburban woods, we followed the dark contours of the city's reservoir lake, working west and north until the elevation began to rise, slightly, into the foothills of the Ouachita Mountains. There we heard a Whip-poor-will, the second of three nightjars found in Arkansas. The Whip-poor-will was the last nocturnal species we'd claim, because just as we heard it, its name-repeating song was joined by the chip notes of Northern Cardinals, Tufted Titmice calling from the oaks, and Carolina Chickadees welcoming the day. The dawn chorus had begun, and the slow start of night birding turned to the rapid tallying of daytime species.

We followed the road back toward the lake, the windows rolled down. As Ari drove slowly enough that we could hear, we tallied the birds—Eastern Phoebe, Pine Warbler, Eastern Bluebird. With the light still low, we didn't even bother looking; the birds were letting us know they were there through their sounds.

When we arrived back at the lake's western edge, we pulled into a park called Vista Point. During the winter, this is a favorite place for ducks, grebes, and loons, and it often boasts a wide variety of species and more than a few rare birds. By this time in the spring, most of the wintering ducks and waterbirds had moved north, but there was still the hope of a tern migrating through or a loon lingering on the water.

It was there by the lake that we saw the sunrise, a glowing red sky in the east. It was a sky like none I'd ever seen, the red nearly as bright as a Cardinal's. We all knew the warning the color carried: "Red sky at morning, sailor's warning," the adage goes. It names the truth that a red dawn is often an indication of high water content in the air and a low-pressure system approaching. Storms were coming. The forecast on our phones reflected the same warning. Rain was on its way, and soon.

We had known that this was a possibility. With a pick of days for our birding, we'd settled on this one because it worked for our schedules and coincided with peak migration. But weather is hard to plan for. Even when we saw the chance of rainstorms in the morning, we decided to go ahead anyway. Rain can be a mixed reality for birding. During a hard downpour, there's not much to see, but after it passes, rain can create the conditions for a fallout—a time when rain or strong north winds force birds to stop flying and seek shelter in trees or shrubs. As the storm clouds gathered, however, we felt less certain about the promise of that plan. We had to make the most of the time before the rain began falling.

At another pullout by the lake, we followed a short trail around the water's edge. Soon we heard a call, familiar, and yet one none of us could identify for certain. This happens every spring for me. Birds whose calls I know, but only hear at certain times of year, always require a refresher. For the weeks before this Big Day I'd been practicing with "The Warbler Guide" app, one of the most useful birding apps created. It is a version of *The Warbler Guide* book, a species guide that was revolutionary when it came out due to its use of sonograms. By visualizing bird songs at the same time as hearing them, its authors contended, we can better learn the songs.

What we were hearing now, however, was no warbler. The song was a jumble of notes, one that none of us could quite place. It was then that one of us pulled out a phone and opened the Merlin app.

I began birding in the analog age. If you wanted to know what bird was singing, you had to go find it, watch it sing, and work to remember it for the future. There were CDs I'd play on the boom box in my room to train my ear, but that training was of limited use. Really learning bird songs mostly required patient presence in the field.

Merlin, created by the Cornell Lab of Ornithology, has significantly changed that. Merlin began as a sort of field guide for beginners. It would walk birders through a process of elimination, starting with size and shape, moving to color, and then providing some possible matches for the bird in front of them.

Then, Merlin introduced a sound ID tool, through which you could record a bird call and the app would identify it. Quickly, this became Merlin's most popular feature. A birder can hold their phone up to a chorus of singing birds and report back what is in the mix. "Hearing a bird," the Merlin app reports, as it begins recording a sonogram. If the sound is strong enough and the conditions right, it will match it to one of thousands of species in its database.

At its best, Merlin acts like a good birder friend—someone who can help to tune you in to what is singing around you. It can confirm a hunch or give a clue for further investigation. But like so much technology, Merlin can also disrupt the work of listening, interrupting the direct line between the birder and the bird. If not used with care, Merlin can not only misidentify a bird, it can also keep birders from learning the birds on their own. I've seen birders blithely add birds identified by Merlin to their checklists without bothering to even confirm the species themselves. When several birds are calling at once, they don't know which ones are which. They only know that Merlin heard a White-throated Sparrow, and a Robin, and a Cardinal.

When I began birding, I read this advice: Watch the bird, pay attention to its plumage, its behavior, its shape, and its song. See what kind of habitat it prefers, what other birds it associates with. Only then—only *after* all that—turn to a field guide.

I think the same sort of advice could be used for Merlin. Make it a reference, a tool, but don't let it replace your work of listening. "Hearing a bird"—this should begin with you.

Hearing was what we were doing with this bird in the Sweet Gums, its song a melodic mess. Merlin reported back: Orchard Oriole. Oh yes, we all agreed. That was it, the name on the tip of our tongues. The habitat was right, as was the season, and soon the burnt orange and black bird came into view. The next time we heard it, we'd know it.

"Hear O Israel"—this is the beginning call of the Shema, the central prayer of Judaism. The name of the prayer, *shema*, is in fact the Hebrew word for "hear." It could be said, then, that the central statement of Judaism is "The Hear."

To hear is different than to read. The act of common hearing has a way of forming a people, making a community. I knew a Navajo woman once, an Episcopal priest, and she talked about the essence of her people being held in songs and stories. These weren't simply artifacts of culture for her—they were like animate agents, auditory spirits that held the very life of her people. And so it was, and has continued to be, for the Jewish people.

In my own church tradition, a lector reads Scripture aloud to the congregation each Sunday. And though the texts being read are printed in our bulletins, I avoid following along with the printed passage. Whether it is read well or mumbled, I always work to listen, and thus to hear the word of Scripture. It does something different to hear the Word. Listening to the Scriptures has a formative effect, a way of making us into a community, that reading the text on our own does not.

Author readings are a secular version of this. I love to hear a writer I admire read their own work, especially a poet. I've had the opportunity to hear several great poets: from N. Scott Momaday to Grace Paley, Amiri Baraka to Li-Young Lee. There is a kind of collective experience that comes from this common hearing, a unique instantiation of a reality in a particular moment that will never happen again in quite the same way. The text will remain, but that particular reading of it was etched into that unique place and time.

The same is true of a symphony or any live music. Beethoven's Ninth Symphony has not changed in a century, but each performance of it is different due to the space in which it is played, the instruments involved, and the people listening and playing. Each time I hear a robin sing I am hearing familiar music, but it is sound captured in this unique moment. This kind of listening in the unique instances of life is what true hearing is all about.

Sounds have their seasons and seasons their sounds. The rise and fall of the Blue Grosbeak's song is a key to my own sense of summer. The males of these birds are a dark blue, while the females are a peanut-butter brown. Their melodic song is one I heard through my young birding days, and a green pasture and warm afternoon still bring it to mind in expectation. A newly returned Blue Grosbeak sang from the brushy edge of the lake levee. It was joined in song by its relative, the brighter and smaller Indigo Bunting.

Up the hill we heard the drumming of a woodpecker on a tree. This too was a call. We think of bird songs and calls in terms of their vocalizations, but some birds belong to the percussion section of the soundscape. Woodpeckers drum against trees in search of insects, but they also use their drumming as a means of communication. Many homeowners will learn this fact when a woodpecker—often the ground-feeding, suburb-loving Northern Flicker—discovers a particularly resonant piece of flashing or a rain gutter to pound on. Each morning those living in the home will be greeted by a loud banging, which is just the male flicker's way of announcing his claim on that territory and his availability as a mate. The more hollow and resonant the object, the farther the sound will reach. If the male successfully attracts a mate with a particular drum, he will return to it year after year.

Other birds, like Ruffed Grouse, drum on fallen logs with their wings, and some species of flycatchers make snapping sounds with their bills. The range of bird sound communication is broad. What is necessary is listening to it.

Psychologists and artists alike are working to make deep listening a deliberate practice. Among them is D. Graham Burnett, a writer and historian who helped found the "Friends of Attention," a loose collective of real friends who have committed themselves to the work of "attention activism." They focus on the "the promotion of human flourishing in direct response to the commodification of human attention." One outgrowth of this group is the Strother School of Radical Attention, in which classes are gathered to engage in collective acts of looking and listening.

I love work of this kind. And it is what happens every time I go birding. A Big Day could be reframed as an outing of radical attention, a course in deep listening. The world around us is alive with sounds and sights that are subtle and beautiful, but we have blocked these out through the protective reaction of broad-spectrum defenses. Going out to the quieter places of city edges and parks, or the fields and forests of rural areas that have not yet been overrun by constant machines, we can join in listening to the creatures that share our world and want to be heard—at least by one another if not by us.

It is important to remember that when we pay attention to birds, their sounds and their behaviors, we are not simply hearing a pleasant noise, some ambient music for the ecological landscape. We are encountering an act of communication. Birds are constantly telling one another about what is happening in the world and communicating their intentions for it. The Blue Grosbeak was likely setting up a nesting territory, the reach of his song a declaration of its borders. There was also a female close by, so perhaps he was trying to get her attention. Like all communication, bird talk carries multiple meanings.

Animal trackers, particularly Indigenous trackers whose livelihood depends upon following animals, are tuned in to the more subtle communications of birds. The documentarian Craig Foster, for instance, speaks of following a J'honsi tracker in the Kalahari. The ability of this tracker to stay with an animal seemed at first like magic. And yet as Foster learned his methods, he found that the tracker was paying attention to what birds were telling him about where large animals were. "A little bird told me" is a coy old trope; but for many humans past and present, it is more than mere metaphor.

Many of us who pursue the hobby of birding spend too little time listening in this way. We seek to identify birds, in all their varieties, and once the box is checked we move on. Jon Young, an animal-tracking teacher and birder, knows the impulse. In his book *What the Robin Knows*, he invites us to slow down and pay attention to not only what species a bird is but what it reveals about the world around it. "If we learn to read the birds—and their behaviors and vocalizations—through them, we can read the world at large," writes Young. Too often, he says, we simply collide with birds, their world and ours meeting for a passing instant. "[I]f we replace collision with connection, learn to read these details, feel at home, relax, and are respectful," he writes, "ultimately the birds will yield to us the first rite of passage: a close encounter with an animal otherwise wary of our presence."

I had these kinds of close encounters as a child with endless time to spend exploring the woods, a time before I had access to a car and speed and the ability to travel far in search of birds. I would simply go to the woods to explore, often sitting quietly to watch the world of the forest move around me. Now, well into middle age, I'm returning to this childhood practice. I've had plenty of time to chase species, and though I still enjoy it, as a Big Day no doubt reveals, I spend far more of my birding time going deep in the communities of life that share my home landscape. By listening there, I am learning to hear the world at large.

As we walked along the levee, the birds suddenly fell quiet after a burst of song. It didn't take the advanced skills of a tracker to understand why. Dark clouds were rolling in, along with the rumble of thunder. Rain was coming quickly, and we had no desire to be standing in an open space by water when the lightning arrived. We rushed back down the hill to Ari's car just in time to escape the deluge.

On a Big Day there's always a plan, a route organized with rough times outlined for each stop. And then there are the conditions of the day itself.

As the rain proved to be more than a passing shower, David and I opened our phones as Ari steered through the flooding streets. It appeared that south of town the rain was lighter. We had planned to bird that area toward the end of our Big Day. But looking at the hourly forecast, we decided to follow our route in reverse, hoping that we would end up with more dry hours for birding.

Following the interstate south and east of Little Rock, we eventually found ourselves at the Arkansas Game and Fish Commission's

Delta Rivers Nature Center. As we opened our doors in the parking area, we were met with the sound of Barred Owls, mixed with the deep growls of bullfrogs and the singing of crickets. We needed a Barred Owl for our list. But the joke was on us: The sound was coming from the building's speakers, which blasted the sounds of nature into the bottomland woods around it.

I understood the desire to provide an experience of nature for visitors, school buses full of children unlikely to find a real owl or hear a bullfrog on an hour-long visit, but it reminded me of persistent problem in modern life: We want a guaranteed experience rather than the chance of a surprise encounter.

In his book, *On the Uncontrollability of the World*, the German sociologist Hartmut Rosa writes that we experience our deepest human meanings in what he calls resonance. Resonance is "a kind of relationship to the world . . . in which subject and world are mutually affected and transformed. . . . Resonance is not an echo, but a responsive relationship, requiring that both sides speak with their own voice." We long for this resonance and yet, Rosa says, it cannot be manufactured. Like an elusive bird, it flies when we try to capture it. Despite this, much of modern life is an attempt to create a reliable experience of resonance. We go to a nature center, a museum, a church, not on the chance that we may encounter wonder, but with an expectation that we will be provided with an experience. Rosa writes that the greatest fear of the modern age is "fear of the world's falling mute." And yet, by seeking to make the world more controllable by making resonance a reliable experience, "Modernity stands at risk of *no longer hearing the world*." "Modernity," writes Rosa, "has lost its ability to be *called*, to be *reached*."

After a quick bathroom break, we walked away from the nature center, out of earshot of the recorded calls, and as we did, true resonance awaited. It began slowly along the trail that brought us into the bottomland hardwoods, typical of this delta ecoregion of Arkansas. Tall trees, including cottonwoods and water oaks, were mixed with huge vines of wild grape. The understory was a mix of hawthorn and other small trees, all sparse, the undergrowth kept at bay by regular flooding. The rain had mostly stopped, and the sound of slowly dripping water echoed across the canopy as the water made its gravity-guided journey toward the ground.

A Wood Thrush sang its ethereal, otherworldly song from a low perch, while Baltimore Orioles chattered from high up, their bright orange flashing among the fresh spring leaves. From a vine, an Eastern Wood-pewee gave its eponymous whistle, and everywhere there seemed to be a *chip*, a rustle, a movement. Something was afoot. We all felt a tingling: the energy that experienced birders can feel, that we were about to walk into something special.

Our hopes for the rain had come true—we had just walked into a small fallout of migrating songbirds. Forced to the ground by the storm, these warblers, thrushes, tanagers, and orioles were now gorging themselves on what seemed to be a flush of caterpillars. Every bird we got our binoculars on had a caterpillar hanging from its beak. The timing of migration, at least in these woods, had been just right—providing an abundance of food at just the right time and place.

Around a bend in the trail, we saw a thrush hop from the path. It was a light, uniform rusty brown. Veery! we called to each other. This is not a rare migrant, but also not the most abundant. I had passed plenty of springs in Arkansas without encountering one. The bird hopped from the path onto a low branch and cocked its head, clearly listening to us as we approached.

We often forget that, just as we give our attention to birds, birds are also listening to us. Just as the watchers become the watched, the listeners become the listened to. Birds have excellent senses. Most species have excellent vision, with a range of color that goes beyond the human eye. They can also hear well, often picking up on pitches beyond our perception. And though it was once thought that many birds do not have an advanced sense of smell, new research is beginning to challenge that belief. With all these senses they are paying attention to the deep currents of the world around them, somehow even sensing phenomena that we would think impossible to predict.

This bird before us, the Veery, can somehow sense hurricanes months in advance. Researchers have no idea how, but Veerys clearly time their migrations based on the severity of hurricane season in the Atlantic. In 2018, Delaware State University ornithologist Dr. Christopher Heckscher demonstrated this by beating most meteorologists in predicting the severity of the hurricane season. All he did was pay attention to what the Veerys were doing in their migration. Perhaps meteorologists, for all their advanced technologies, should work more like traditional trackers and ask the birds what's happening.

Beyond the Veery we heard the *sweet-sweet-sweet* song of the Prothonotary Warbler, the rising note of an Indigo Bunting, and the fast-paced *ta-ta-ta-ta-tattt* of the Tennessee Warbler. The more we moved into the woods, the more intense the sounds of the birds became. As we turned the bend that moved us back toward the visitor center, we found a tree buzzing with birds, Chestnut-sided Warblers, with their squeaky wheel song, and Blue-winged Warblers, with their old man snores. The variety, both in sound and sight, was overwhelming, and we added species to our totals, left and right, front and back.

We hated to leave, but a Big Day means moving through as many habitats as possible, and we needed to go east to see and hear entirely different kinds of birds.

From the lowland forest, we drove across the Arkansas River and into the empty wasteland of plowed fields, bare as any desert. This tragic expanse of industrial agriculture was no place for life, and the few birds we encountered were evidence of the poverty of plowed fields.

Here and there House Sparrows sat on power lines and small flocks of Red-winged Blackbirds flew across the expanse, never settling. "Iron Hawk," David joked, pointing at an airplane approaching a field. It swooped low, releasing a spray of chemicals across the ground. Given the season, these were likely pre-emergent herbicides to keep weeds at bay before the primary crop is planted. Born from the chemical warfare operations of the twentieth century's wars, herbicides, pesticides, and nitrogen fertilizers have all aided the consolidation of farming into the hands of a few large operators. "Get big or get out," was the catchphrase of the charismatic deputy secretary of agriculture, Earl Butz, in the 1970s. It was a mantra that left thousands of farm families scrambling to survive. The only way to do so was to turn to the chemical methods of the so-called Green Revolution—a form of agriculture that brought a rapid increase in crop yields while poisoning ecological health. It was with this agricultural revolution that a new reality became threateningly real: a deadening silence.

In her classic 1962 book *Silent Spring*, Rachel Carson opens with "A Fable for Tomorrow," in which she paints the picture of a rural community in which suddenly "There was a strange stillness. . . . It was spring without voices. On the mornings that had once throbbed with the dawn chorus of robins, catbirds, doves, jays, wrens and scores of other bird voices there was now no sound; only silence lay over the fields and woods and marsh."

Carson's book brought to light the particular dangers of DDT, a pesticide whose use was eventually banned because of her work. But her warnings about chemical agriculture and habitat loss were not limited to one pesticide. It is telling that of the species that have been in the sharpest decline over the past fifty years, most have been those that prefer open agricultural areas. The Green Revolution has been anything but.

"Falcon!" Ari called from the driver's seat. Across the horizon we could see the sharp, muscular wing-beats of this alpha predator of the skies. Whenever I'm asked, "what's your favorite bird?" Peregrine Falcon is the answer I give, perhaps due to my boyhood love of the *My Side of the Mountain* series by Jean Craighead George. Despite the desolate waste of plowed fields, this sighting was a bright spot—a new bird for our list and an example of a species who was saved by the work of Carson and others. DDT was particularly harmful to avian predators like falcons and eagles, but since its ban they have returned to healthy populations. Sometimes the silence can call us toward action.

After the long miles of empty roadways, we finally arrived at Bayou Meto Wildlife Management Area, a large patch of wetlands and flooded woods in the heart of the Mississippi Flyway. In the winter, this area is full of both ducks and duck hunters, but well past the season we were here for wading birds and other marshland specialists.

As we drove into the southern part of the refuge, we were greeted by a muddy field hosting hundreds of White-faced Ibis, Little Blue Herons, and a scattering of shorebirds. On the opposite side of the road was a marsh with Common Gallinules and a few American Coots feeding among the vegetation. We set up our scopes and began to work through the mass of birds, hoping to add several new species to help "pay" for miles with no new birds that brought us here.

As we were looking, Ari pointed out a strange sound behind us. It was low and close, a call that seemed more like water running down a drainpipe than anything a bird would make. We stepped away from our scopes and began looking for the source of the sound. As we moved toward the marsh edge, the sound continued, and it seemed so close that it was coming from right in front of our feet. Despite the fact that we were three good birders looking, we couldn't see a bird that was right in front of us. "I think it's an American Bittern," Ari said. I played a recording of the bittern from my phone and there it was—the same water-down-the-drain sound.

A cousin of the Least Bittern I'd encountered on the Texas Coast, the American Bittern is larger and yet more elusive. I've only seen a handful of them. Looking out at the landscape in front of us, we knew that the bittern's camouflage, from its long-necked shape to its brown streaking, would be perfect for this kind of reedy marsh. After looking in vain, we gave up. Hearing the bird was enough to count it, and we couldn't waste too much time trying to see one bird. I, for one, was glad to have heard it, because though I had seen them before, this was the first time I had actually heard the bittern's strange song.

The road into the Wildlife Management Area dead-ended at the Bayou. In the far corner of the field by the turn around we watched a group of Dowitchers feeding. They were far off, and in this time of year both Long-billed and Short-billed Dowitchers could have been present. Distinguishing the two by sight is notoriously difficult, one of the most challenging "ID problems" in birding. But the sound of the two species is distinct. This is true of many bird species groups. Dowitchers, Empidonax flycatchers, Myarchus flycatchers, Yellow-legs—all have species within their genus that can be hard to tell apart by sight alone. But to hear any one of the birds is to get a definitive answer of what kind of bird it is.

I'd hate to give up a sense, but as a birder it would be a hard choice between seeing and hearing. Hearing, certainly, offers a greater diversity of encounter—access to a broader expanse of life. Thankfully, so far at least, I have sharp enough eyes and ears, and I'm doing all in my power to keep it that way.

The journey back toward Little Rock brought a smattering of species—a Barred Owl calling from the dark forest of a bayou, a kingfisher by a roadside ditch, a harrier teetering over a field of Little Bluestem grass— but not enough to push us toward the total we had hoped for. We called the day a bit early, arriving home at dusk. We'd had better lists in past years, and we began discussing missed opportunities and improvements to our route for next year. Yet for all that, we had still spent a day attending to the creatures we love. We'd formed a community made through listening.

6

JUNE

Grief

A BARRED OWL dipped above my car, angling into the cypress bayou beside the road, as I looked down at the glowing map on my phone. Last year I had dropped a pin so I could find my way back to the start: a bend on a dirt road in the Arkansas delta. It was 5:20 a.m., and in exactly six minutes I would begin my most scientific birding excursion of the year: running my BBS route.

The North American Breeding Bird Survey is a project operated by the United States Geological Survey in conjunction with partner agencies in Canada and Mexico. Through data collected by experienced birders, the BBS has provided some of the best information we have on the state of North American birds—changes in distribution, which birds are in decline, and which species are on the rise. Some birders have multiple routes they run in the late spring and early summer. I can only manage one route, and I do it just east of where I live.

The survey is set up as a classic "point count," with fifty stops along a specified route. At each stop, the observer is to step outside the car and count every bird seen or heard for three minutes. When the timer ends, so does the counting. This sort of data collection is the gold standard for bird species surveys. I have increasingly felt an obligation to use my birding skills to help scientists better understand bird population trends. Birding is a joy, and I've known birders who won't do surveys like this because they can become monotonous. But committing one morning each June to this route has become for me an act of mundane devotion.

I began running BBS routes as a teenager, as soon as I was able to drive myself to the remote starting points on rural roads. I got pulled over more than once by small-town police officers, who wanted to know what a teenager was doing out at 4 a.m. When I explained that I was on my way to conduct a survey of breeding birds, they let me off on the grounds that no kid could make that up on the spot.

Now, in middle age, I have fewer run-ins with the police. Still, a guy driving along, stopping every quarter mile, and looking around with binoculars, does draw attention. The local Audubon Society printed up some nice car door magnets that say "Volunteer Bird Survey" to help. I also make sure to wear a yellow safety vest and keep a clipboard in hand to make me look more official.

So with magnets on my car and vest on my back, I was ready when the time came: 5:26 a.m., thirty minutes before sunrise. I opened my eBird app and began counting. Cardinals and Indigo Buntings, both loud dawn choristers, were the first on the list. Then, faintly, in the distance I heard the lazy warble of a Blue Grosbeak interspersed with the trill of Red-winged Blackbirds. I listened carefully, adding numbers to each species, while keeping an eye on the time as it crept toward three minutes. Right on the minute I stopped the list as the sky began to glow with rose in the east.

I remember little of what I saw on those teenage BBS excursions; still, they mark a history of watching. I've been birding for over three decades. To have such a long experience means that I've seen changes in bird populations—the rise and fall of species. There's a line in Shakespeare's *King Lear* in which the young Edgar speaks of being "'Twixt two extremes of passion, joy and grief." This describes the birder's life in this time, the life of anyone who loves the wild world. There is joy in it, wonder and great beauty. Just to see an Indigo Bunting is a thing of amazement—the radiant blue of the males, iridescent in the sun; the soft secret brown of the females, tending their nests in thickets along the road. But I know that there are fewer Indigo Buntings now than when I began birding thirty years ago. They are a bird in decline. And that knowledge brings with it grief.

The headline of a 2019 study that caught the attention of the world was "3 Billion North American Birds Lost Since 1970." The study, which analyzed a wide array of data, including from the Breeding Bird Survey, showed that many species, even common birds like Blue Jays, are in a steep decline. Together, we've lost 30 percent of the total bird population. The causes for this loss, the researchers speculated, were varied. Habitat loss, outdoor cats, and window strikes were among the leading culprits.

In the end, however, underlying them all is the totalizing human presence upon the earth—one that excludes other creatures from sharing in our common life. That reality, for all those who care about nonhuman life, is a thing of deep sadness.

The road continued around a series of bends, through a field of young sorghum and soybeans. The irrigation ditches hosted unmowed berms where most birds were active: Red-winged Blackbirds nesting in the low shrubs, a Common Yellowthroat singing from a patch of cattails. Eventually, I came to a stop described by the researcher who created this route as "100 yards before telephone pole with two transformers." I'd grown up with these landmark-based rural directions. They can seem vague, even unhelpful, but it was clear enough as I came around the corner. On the south side of the road, opposite a field of young soybeans, there was an oxbow lake full of cypress trees. The water from the oxbow was being pumped into the fields, but it didn't seem to have hurt the large stand of cypress.

Bayou, oxbow—these are among the unique landscape words of my region, links to both the culture and hydrology of the place. I like to use them because they reflect an affection for the particulars, a tie to a history that reaches back to the Choctaw, whose word for a slow-moving stream was adopted by the French of Louisiana and then by others in the region to become *bayou*.

An oxbow refers to the u-shaped piece of metal that helped hold a yoke to an ox for plowing. The shape was what came to mind when early mapmakers sought to describe lakes made of river bends that had become disconnected from the original course.

Learning to name the features of a place and its creatures is a part of belonging to it. But many of the unique names for wild places and things are being lost, replaced by the uniform terms of a mass culture and the vocabularies of technology.

It was this loss that inspired the writer Robert MacFarlane to compose his beautiful books of poems, *Lost Words* and *Lost Spells*. When the *Oxford Junior Dictionary* withdrew words for the natural world and replaced them with words for digital technology, MacFarlane and others experienced a kind of grief. Words are ways of knowing and encounter. To say "cardinal," "chickadee," "junco" is to have a different depth of understanding, an intricacy of relationship, not possible by just saying "bird." When we forget the particular words for places and creatures, then our connection to them suffers a loss. I want my daughters to not only know *swamp* but also *bayou*. I want them to know what it means for a lake to be an oxbow and all the hydrological history encapsulated in that term.

Here the oxbow was dense with cypress trees, their trunks massive, surrounded by the knobby "knees" that make them so distinct. No one knows the purpose of these knees, only that they are more common among cypress that grow in deep water. Some believe they help bring air to the roots of the trees, or help prevent erosion, or perhaps they have a combination of functions. I am always glad when some phenomenon so common is still mysterious. Knowledge is a wonder, but we can be tempted to think we know far more than we do. An everyday mystery can humble us.

From the depths of the cypress, I could hear the *sweet-sweet-sweet* song of the Prothonotary Warbler. These are one of the two

North American Warblers that nest in tree cavities. Bright yellow with soft gray wings, Prothonotary Warblers can be found in cypress stands and flooded forests throughout the summer in Arkansas. And though their habitat preferences are specific, their populations are thankfully stable.

When I stand by a forest like this, however, I can't help but think about those birds that haunt it. I recently participated in a community art project—a weaving together of grief. Most resonant for me was that for each movement of the weaving, Patti, our leader, played the song of a different ghost bird—a species that had gone extinct. Among them was the song of the Bachman's Warbler, a species that was never well studied before it was last seen in the early 1960s. It would have nested in Arkansas, in the shrubby undergrowth of bottomland forests. A Bachman's Warbler could well have been present, a century ago, along the route of my Breeding Bird Survey.

More well known was another bird whose calls Patti played—the Ivory-billed Woodpecker. Blurry images and the accounts of ornithologists have kept the hope alive that somewhere, somehow, a population is still surviving. But there has been frustratingly little clear documentation. Arkansas has been at the center of such possibilities. But with scant evidence after a massive search, many have given up hope. These woodpeckers, known as the "Good Lord Bird!" for the exclamation they once evoked with their magnificent size and sudden appearance, are likely extinct or nearly so.

The loss, in the end, came down to sewing machines.

By the 1940s, Ivory-billed Woodpeckers were in trouble. Each pair required an estimated 2.5 acres of old-growth forest to survive, and with increased logging such tracts of forest were fewer and fewer. The woodpeckers were starving in much of their range, except for a large woodland that stretched from East Texas to Louisiana. That forest was purchased by the Singer Sewing Company, which wanted the lumber for making sewing-machine cabinets. Singer sold the logging and milling rights to the Chicago Mill and Lumber Company.

Using German POWs as laborers, the Chicago Mill Company clear-cut the entire forest, despite an offer by the United States government of $200,000 (a very large sum at the time) to make the area a national park for the protection of the Ivory-billed Woodpecker. Singer and the Chicago Mill stood to make more money by cutting the timber, so they made that choice. James Griswold, the chair of the Chicago Mill and Lumber board, couldn't have stated it more plainly: "We are just money grubbers. We are not concerned, as are you folks, with ethical considerations."

And with that, the last universally accepted sighting of an Ivory-billed Woodpecker came in April 1944 by Audubon Society artist Don Eckelberry, who documented the birds as the last of the trees were being cut.

At the same gathering where I had listened to the sounds of ghost birds, I heard a presentation by theologian Hannah Malcom. Malcom is an English priest and scholar who has written elegantly on the practice of grief in the face of the climate crisis. We tend to think about grief as an emotion, a response to some tragedy or loss. But Malcom argues that grief can also be a deliberate practice, one that forms our ethical responses to the world around us. Malcom frames this practice around a question posed by the philosopher Judith Butler: Which bodies are grievable? For Butler, the question of grievability defines the value we offer to a life. "Precisely because a living being may die, it is necessary to care for that being so that it may live," writes Butler. "Only under conditions in which the loss would matter does the value of the life appear. Thus, grievability is a presupposition for the life that matters."

We grieve the loss of friends more than strangers, the death of a child more than an elder. A death in the family, even someone who lived at a geographic distance, often disturbs our life far more than a neighbor. Butler's question points us toward an honest assessment of who receives our grief. We are willing, for the sake of stability, security, and some idea of progress, to sacrifice some bodies while grieving others. Ultimately, the question of grief is a question of love. Who and what we love is essentially the same question as who and what we mourn.

To understand Butler's challenge in terms of the natural world, consider the darter fish. On summer days, when my family gets the chance, we leave the city behind and drive to the Ouachita National Forest to our west. There is a hidden trail that leads to a swimming hole only a few people know about. It has even escaped, so far, the all-seeing eye of Google Maps. The pool isn't large, but it is deep enough for an adult to be fully submerged, and it is spring-fed with cool water even after weeks without rain.

On a recent visit, I stood on the shallow side as my daughters played in the deeper water. As I stood there, I watched the creatures moving about in the stream. There were numerous orange crawfish, feeding on the leaves that had settled on the bottom. Smallmouth bass darted here and there, living in the nursery of the stream until a storm will carry them to the larger river downstream. There were insects of various kinds, some balanced in perfect tension on the water's surface, others paddling beneath the surface with feet like oars.

Then, for a moment, I saw a small, slender fish with deep red vents. Without knowing the particular species, I recognized immediately that this was some kind of darter fish. Many species of darter fish are threatened or endangered because they are adapted to live in clean, free-flowing streams. Obstacles, from dams to gravel mines, can significantly impair their habitat.

I had recently listened to an interview with an economist who was explaining, in exasperation, why economic growth has not been as a rapid over the past fifty years as it could have been. Among the reasons, he speculated, were too many environmental regulations. As an example, he named an endangered snail darter fish that had prevented construction of a hydroelectric dam somewhere in the United States. For the economist, the snail darter was not grievable. He would have gladly traded its existence for the economic growth the hydroelectric dam would have provided.

Watching the darter in the creek, bolting from place to place, though, I would have easily traded more economic progress for the continued life of this species. Since the time I was a child, the thought of the loss of any species has been tremendously grievable. But this was true because I had spent so much time in the woods, time in which I had cultivated an affection for wild things. My love for the wild world is far greater than my love for economic growth. And though I know that is a complex position to take, I have tried to make moves throughout my life to stay true to the ordering of those affections.

We have lost the Ivory-billed Woodpecker and the Bachman's Warbler and the Passenger Pigeon and myriad other unique, wild creatures. We lost them because we did not love their presence and thus did not grieve their passing. If we want to live toward a different future, one that is not marked by the arrival of the sixth mass extinction in earth's history, then we must learn the practice of grief as a part of the work of love.

The road curved from the oxbow of cypress and moved toward the tar and gravel surface of a paved highway. The shoulders here weren't wide, and the cars were more frequent, so the prescribed stops were spaced at intervals wherever a car could safely stop. On the data-recording form for the Breeding Bird Survey, in addition to counting the birds present, observers are asked to note how many cars pass during the three minutes of the count, as well as any loud noises that could impede hearing. To this point in the count, I'd marked every stop with a 0, but now that I was on the highway, the totals were reaching three or more cars per stop.

To stand by a roadside with cars whizzing past is to realize that speed carries with it a kind of violence. We don't usually think about this when we're in cars, but traveling at such speeds pushes our bodies to a pace beyond what our senses can process. For the world that stands still or moves along at a slower, creaturely speed, the velocity can prove dangerous and overwhelming. This violence of velocity was clear along this highway, where an array of animal carcasses lined the pavement from the previous night's rush of driving—raccoons with their bandit masks and human-like hands, opossums, those strange North American marsupials, skunks with their bold black and white and musky stench, armadillos, with their protective shells, shattered, not to mention the turtles, snakes, and yes, birds.

Roadkill offers another window into what we consider ungrievable. We pass by the victims, mostly without note or comment. We even make the varied animals killed by cars into a homogenous, generic group through this generalized term: *roadkill.* Children notice, sometimes, calling attention to the grisly carcasses from the backseat. "Yes, it's sad, honey," we say. But eventually they join us in our numbness, rushing along while barely noticing the dead. And yet, for all the mundane macabre nature of roadkill, we must admit that these are the deaths of creatures. Their senseless end came about for no other reason than our need for speed and power.

That same artist who played the songs of ghost birds, Patti Fong, introduced me to the work of Thom van Dooren, a "field philosopher" and head of the Sydney Environment Institute. Van Dooren, especially in his book *The Wake of Crows*, examines the grieving rituals of birds and how they can teach us the work of grief. Crows, and their cousins the magpies, will enact rituals of grieving that only the most mechanistic mind would dismiss. Magpies, a close relative to crows, will gather around a fallen member of their flock, calling out with their heads raised toward the sky, then moving around the body, touching it with their beaks. Search for magpie funerals online and you'll see dozens of examples. These are birds that mourn.

Many birds fall without much more than a passing notice—unless, that is, we decide to pay attention. I have worked for many years in a downtown church, a setting that has given me the opportunity to get to know many people who are unhoused. One man (I'll call him Frank) has been a regular member of my congregation for nearly a decade, off and on. I was visiting with Frank on a spring day when he told me that he finds all kinds of birds dead beneath the tall buildings downtown. These birds are victims of window strikes, one of the deadliest obstacles for the migrating birds that travel over our cities at night. The tall buildings and windows are dangerous enough, but what makes them particularly deadly are the lights in the buildings, which disorient the birds. Policies by cities and building managers to go "lights out" on heavy nights of migration can make for a safer migratory path for birds and significantly reduce the number of confused birds hitting illuminated windows.

When he finds a dead bird on the sidewalk, Frank told me, he picks it up and brings it to a local park. "They're just so beautiful, I hate to leave them there on the sidewalk." He wondered what species each bird was. He wanted to know their stories. I told Frank that the next time he found one, he could bring it to me and I could tell him the species.

A few days after our conversation, Frank came by the church. He had carefully wrapped two birds in paper. The first was a male Indigo Bunting. The second was smaller, with an olive back, yellow throat, and black mask edged with gray. This was a male Common Yellowthroat. Frank gave the birds to me to hold.

It is always a shock, though I've done it hundreds of times, to have a bird in hand. They are so light that their bodies seem almost like an illusion, a trick of perception. With hollow bones and an intricate blend of traits, they are designed to fly.

At my church, we have a memorial garden in a courtyard next to the church where cremated ashes are placed. With a surreptitious glance toward the office to make sure our church administrator didn't see where I was headed, I led Frank into the garden. Beside the roots of an azalea bush, I dug a small hole. We placed the two birds, united by a shared habitat and fate, in the ground, and I asked Frank if he wanted to pray. He led us in the Lord's Prayer. He explained to me that the Our Father was a prayer that had helped him through many difficult times. Then I gave a few words of commendation. Dust to dust is true for birds as much as it is for any of us. We are common creatures of earth.

Common Yellowthroats were among the birds I was hearing now as I moved, stop by stop, down the road. They prefer wet, low-lying brushy edges, and overgrown highway side ditches are perfect hosts. Though they are not always easy to see at first pass, the males sing loudly, proclaiming their territory to all who will listen. They are also one of the species, along with wrens and kinglets, that are the first to arrive when I give a *pishing* call.

Above me, as the day began to warm, I started to see swallows. A large group of them perched on a line along the dirt road I turned on next, all huddled in a row. Most were Northern Rough-winged Swallows, including a few juvenile birds, so these may have included a few family groups. Scattered among them were also some Barn Swallows, beautiful fork-tailed birds that commonly make their mud nests above porch lights. As I approached the designated stop and drove past their perch, they scattered into the air, only to settle again when I was safely past.

Swallows feed on flying insects, of which there are many. As ground-bound animals who tend to notice the large and flashy, we often miss the whole ecosystem in the air above us. From spiders traveling by parachute to small beetles looking for a good garden on which to feast, the world above us is alive. And swallows are among the alpha predators of this airborne world.

Because insects are often nuisances or outright detriments to our own projects, humans are rarely fans of the insect world. I have heard otherwise rational people propose extinction projects for whole categories of insects, like mosquitos. What good are they? Not grievable.

But sometimes we find our way to grief for one thing through another. Birds, in their beauty, their delightful presence, have a better way of catching our sympathy than most insects on which they rely. A spring without bird song was how Rachel Carson presented the apocalyptic future of continued pesticide use. What if there were a spring without swallows?

A few years ago, I read in horror about an episode in which hundreds of White-throated Swifts, a cousin of the swallow, fell from the sky in the Western United States. These birds, on examination, were clearly starving. In a story in the *Guardian*, Martha Desmond, a professor at the University of New Mexico, described finding dozens of warblers, swallows, and flycatchers around her house that had simply fallen from the sky—birds that seemed to be starving. "To see this many individuals and species dying is a national tragedy," she said.

From climate chaos to continued pesticide use, insect populations, especially flying insects, have crashed. When scientists first realized how dire the problem had become, headlines of the coming "insect apocalypse" were made. Insect declines have tracked closely with the declines in bird populations, and the two are likely related.

Apocalypse is a term that gets bandied about a great deal these days. It's a term that came down to most of us through the Bible, where the book of Revelation is also called the Apocalypse. That's because apocalypse is taken from the Greek word for revelation: an unveiling. To have an apocalypse doesn't mean destruction, as we've come to use it, but is instead the uncovering of a hidden truth.

Recognizing, after years of ignoring the problem, the rapid declines of insects and birds and so many other creatures on earth, we are experiencing an apocalyptic moment. The revelation, though, isn't of some divine wrath being meted out but rather of the consequences of human activity on the earth. Especially since the dawn of the Industrial Revolution, we have exploited the earth with ever more rapid extractions of its resources, gaining control over our material lives as never before. Agriculture has become a thing of amazing precision, a reality that will not be so hard to transfer to robots, fulfilling the dreams of science fiction writers like Isaac Asimov. But that control and precision have come at the cost of the world. It is, as it has always been, a Faustian bargain of the most devastating sort.

What to do? There are many and myriad actions. A deindustrialization of agriculture is a start. Focusing on ecological, regenerative forms of farming that work in concert with the whole system of life is an important beginning. But all of this should be rooted in a more difficult task: learning to care for creatures outside our own ends and purposes.

The gravel of the road pinged against the undercarriage of my car as I followed its curves west and then north. When I returned to the pavement, I moved into an area where farmland was giving way to houses with large estates. My next stop, the notes told me, would be opposite a gate whose bricks had the etched title "Promised Land." The road behind the gate curved through an expanse of green, mown grass with a smattering of small trees, leading to a sprawling ranch-style house.

Promised Land: the title of the property caught my attention. The story of gaining and losing the "promised land" in the Bible is one of joy and grief, oscillating through history between the two. What the promised land is, and how we live in it, is a matter of imagination and ethics. This land was a sprawling property, five acres at least, and yet it supported very little life. In his essay "The Gift of Good Land," the writer and farmer Wendell Berry challenges our easy interpretations of claiming a land as our own, promised or not.

In the biblical account, Berry points out, the people of Israel were brought into the land not as owners but as tenants. "The land is mine," said the Lord. The tenants, then, had to work within obligations of use, laws that included giving the land rest, and provisions for making space for wild animals and the landless poor. They were to make room for creation just as God had made room for them. If there was no room for others, for wild creatures, could it really be the promised land?

Wendell Berry at another time wrote in one of his poems: "There are no unsacred places; / there are only sacred places / and desecrated places." Part of the practice of grief is learning to tell the difference between these two. The Promised Land housing development on this oxbow might seem to be a sacred place, even a beautiful one to many. But that would be true only if one refused to grieve those creatures made homeless by its maintenance. This large, manicured lawn could have been a prairie full of wildflowers and nesting birds, buzzing with a host of insects.

Some would say that it is simply a matter of aesthetics here—"to each his own." But I believe that beauty and truth are closely tied together, that what we find beautiful is not only a matter of taste but of value. The practice of grief can be a tool in identifying this goodness. To see a landscape cleared of wild beauty and to grieve that loss is to have our vision formed. We have a responsibility to find the good beautiful. And what could be more true, and good, than a wild field abundant with life?

Down the road from the Promised Land was a house that had followed a different way. There grasses were allowed to grow freely, with little bluestem rising from the ground to give refuge to nesting meadowlarks. It was a savannah landscape, open patches of grass dotted with mature trees—water oaks and a few native pecans. When I stopped there to do my three-minute count, I heard one of the most welcome songs of the day—a rising whistle of *bob-bob-white.*

Growing up in the rural pasturelands of Arkansas and Texas, I was familiar with this one. The song, if not the sight, of the Northern Bobwhite Quail was so common as to be almost unremarkable. But in my lifetime Bobwhites have experienced a precipitous decline. Data provided from the North American Breeding Bird Survey demonstrated that the Northern Bobwhite Quail declined by 85 percent between 1966 and 2014. This is a rapid and steep drop in the population of a common bird.

The decline echoes the rise of large-scale industrial agriculture, which led to both habitat loss and increased pesticide use, both of which are believed to be major contributors in the decline. When farmlands no longer allow for brushy edges, or when suburban developments take over farmlands, Bobwhites no longer have a place to nest and forage. But Bobwhite Quail do, as the American Bird Conservancy notes, "respond positively and quickly to habitat management changes on working lands." This means that efforts toward habitat improvement are quick to help restore Bobwhite populations. A project in Oklahoma and Texas called the Oaks and Prairies Joint Venture is working to restore exactly the kind of savannah habitat this yard hosts. Through this project and others like it, Bobwhites and other open-land birds have a hope for the future.

As I continued along the route, the day grew in its heat. June in Arkansas is hot, a place where the word *sweltering* finds its true meaning. High humidity and heat combine so that a step beyond the doors comes with an immediate soaking of sweat. This summer was set to be the hottest on record globally, following records set the year before and the year before that. By 10 a.m., many of the birds I saw were standing, open-mouthed, panting.

Climate grief is a particular form of grief, one that can be overwhelmed by a sense of futility or the bargaining of a manic drive toward solutions. There is knowledge in this grief, an awareness that we are responsible and yet cannot right the wrongs we've committed. And yet another aspect of the grief is this: that we are attached to our wrongs, that we do not know or want to live without them. I was, after all, driving along in a gas-burning car. And I have, on occasion, traveled long distances by air to see the very wild that is destroyed by such acts.

Wendell Berry names the central challenge we all face: "The great obstacle is simply this, the conviction that we cannot change because we are dependent on what is wrong. But that is the addict's excuse, and we know that it will not do."

I recently sat with a man, emaciated, his teeth rotting, his eyes wild with need. I've known him for nearly a decade, and in that time I've also come to recognize that he is a drug addict. He had come by my church in search of money, cash he said he needed for an ID. I offered, as I usually do in such cases, to directly fill the need. I'd gladly go with him to the DMV, pay the fee, and help him get his ID. But, as I suspected, this would not do. He needed cash not for an ID but to pay the cost of an "angry fix," as Alan Ginsberg put it. I told him that I knew his need and what he really wanted and that I'd be glad to help him get free. He stormed out, angry.

There is grief and sorrow in addiction, an undoing of anyone claimed by its grip. To be an addict is a grievous thing. Yet as Berry so sharply points out, we are all addicts to a way gone deeply wrong, a way that is undoing not only our own bodies but the very world of the good creation of which we are members.

In Luke 18, Jesus tells a story of a despised tax collector and well-respected religious leader both praying in the Temple. The religious leader is self-satisfied, giving thanks to God that he is not a sinner like the tax collector. The tax collector, on the other hand, is filled with sorrow, ready to throw himself on God's mercy. "Which one," Jesus asks, "left the temple justified?" The Greek word here is *diakosune*, a term that can mean justified or righteous. There is a sense in this word not of fulfilling some abstract code but of relationship. To be righteous, declared justified, is to be restored to the circle of connection.

Being outside this circle is the source of real grief, and to be brought back in is the source of authentic joy. No one grieves an act of jaywalking, or any act that doesn't harm relationship. The real poison of any wrong is the way it breaks connection with others. As the writer Elizabeth Oldfield defines it: "Sin is disconnection."

It is a broken relationship with the whole of life, with the rest of creation, that is the true source of our condition. Carbon counts are just abstract measures. To know our problem, we need more than measures of the rise in temperatures. We need to recognize the deeper rupture, the division and exclusion, the break of our friendship with the wider, wild world. What we must do, in the face of such grief, is to be like the tax collector—to admit our powerlessness rather than grasp for solutions, to call for mercy instead of holding out for tomorrow's act of genius.

This is the point at which we begin to reach toward humility, the virtue that is the true grounding of who we are as humans. Until we find our roots in the earth, the low places from which we grow, we will not truly, fully, begin to find other possibilities for our life. Grief is a call to bring us down, back to the soil—dust and ashes are an expression of loss, but they are also good ground for a new beginning.

The route map brought me to a turn, leading me back toward the city. The final stops were in a newly built suburb, rows of single-story brick homes, in the treeless expanse of old agricultural fields. New houses and new roads, the rumble of passing cars, their noise drowning out the sounds of birds. I marked "excessive noise" on the form and moved on. At the final stop, just across a busy intersection, I searched for a place to park. The road had often been closed due to flooding, but it was rebuilt now without a shoulder. I drove on, just past the usual count stop and pulled into the drive of an electrical substation. On either side of the road was a marshy woodland, a remnant that refused to be tamed. Water, thankfully, retains a power that remains difficult to control.

Cars passed as I pulled out my phone and started the three-minute timer. The loudest birds were the first I heard, Northern Cardinals and a Tufted Titmouse, then I saw a male Indigo Bunting, iridescent in the sun. It was a bird of beauty, and that sense of its fullness, its wonder, called to my heart. There was, for all the heat and noise and exhaustion of my attention, a flame of something else, a realization of love.

7

JULY

Beauty

SHE'S PERCHED ON a narrow branch, dead and leafless, the iridescence of her back flashing green in the early light. Emily and I sit, our coffee mugs on a small table between us, watching as she moves quickly to chase another bird from the feeder hanging before us. It's hummingbird season, our favorite part of summer.

They have been here, in the state, since spring. The first arrivals came in April, "home" (to us) from their winter in the Yucatan. In my urban yard, however, the Ruby-throated Hummingbirds don't arrive with any regularity until later in the summer, after they've raised their young in the deeper woods. First we have hatch-year juveniles, the males with tiny feathers of red on their gorgets, like the peach-fuzz beards of high-school boys. Then the adults arrive, having finished raising their second and final brood, each pair giving the world four new hummingbirds over the summer. With the demands of nesting over, where insects and spiders are essential for feeding young, the hummingbirds find the abundant flowers and sugar-water feeders of the city a welcome vacation ground before their return south.

Hummingbirds are the gems of the bird world—small and dazzling. Indeed, when people have wanted to name hummingbirds, they have reached for the names of precious stones: ruby, beryl, emerald, topaz, amethyst. In Arkansas we have, at least commonly, only one species of hummingbird, but areas of the Southwestern

United States can have half a dozen. In the Latin American tropics, there are far more. I've sat at Ramsey Canyon in southeast Arizona and watched as a host of species came to the feeders, from the large and aptly named Blue-throated Mountain Gem to the tiny, flame-throated Lucifer Hummingbird. Still, the chance to watch our resident Ruby-throated Hummingbirds offers more than enough beauty to satisfy.

Beauty is part of what attracts us to birds. Whether it is the subtle rainbow sheen on the neck of a Mourning Dove in the full sun or the surprising blue and orange of a male American Kestrel, the bold crimson, white, and black of a male Rose-breasted Grosbeak or the golden eye of a Rusty Blackbird—birds are beautiful creatures.

Even our most common, everyday birds are sublime wonders if we keep our eyes open. A colleague once texted me that she'd just seen the most amazingly beautiful bird right outside her car. She described a bird so wonderful I thought it might be an escaped parrot. She then texted back that the Merlin app told her it was a European Starling, which many consider little more than an avian rat. Seen in full sun, though, their black feathers turning to iridescent rainbows, even these "trash" birds are beautiful.

And all this is just to speak of bird plumages. Their movements in flight, the elaborate courtship displays in which they dance on land, water, and sky, the music of their songs—birds exude beauty in the whole of their being. Because of this, birds have been the inspiration for poetic odes and symphonic rhapsodies; they are the subjects of paintings and sculptures and films. To see birds is to witness freedom, and grace, and power, and we want to be as close to it as possible, to reproduce it as best we can.

As Elaine Scarry writes in *On Beauty and Being Just*: "Beauty brings copies of itself into being. It makes us draw it, take photographs of it, or describe it to other people." Thumb back through the pages of this book, and you'll find that I've often sought to capture, in some feeble way, the beauty of the creatures I'm describing. I want, with words, to share the beauty of the birds I've encountered. Beauty invites sharing. We experience it, and we want others to join us in the wonder. When my wife recently saw a rainbow in a grocery store parking lot, she walked around pointing it out to everyone she passed. I can't help but do the same when I see the beauty of a bird.

With the advent of digital cameras and greater accessibility to high-quality telephoto lenses, bird photography has become a central pursuit for many birders. I know birders who look through their camera lenses as often as through their binoculars. On our online birding forum for Arkansas birds, there's a whole channel dedicated to the sharing of photographs. Why? Because each time we go into the field we see something beautiful, and we want to share it. None of these bird photographers are professionals, and often the images they share are of common birds. But in sharing those photographs, they are following this dictate that beauty seeks to be repeated.

And yet we seem almost embarrassed by our thrall to beauty. We seek to explain it away, noting all the ways it is useful for this or that. One evening my family sat down to watch the Sir David Attenborough documentary *Dancing with the Birds*. Focused on the Birds of Paradise of Papua New Guinea, the film shows some of the most stunning birds in the world, performing elaborate displays of movement, song, and plumage that were by turns amazing and comical. My family, who generally tolerate my love of birding but are not birders themselves, were all taken by these beautiful birds. No sooner had we settled into our wonder at the strange and amazing creatures on the screen than Attenborough interrupted with explanations, attempting to domesticate the wild excesses by boiling it all down to evolutionary strategies of survival. This beauty, for all its absurd wonder, came down to attracting a mate.

Evolution and adaptation have their place, and if understood in their fullness, they can be sources of beauty themselves. Yet as a total explanation, they leave us wanting more. Our hearts rebel against such a reduction of beauty to scientific rationale, what the philosopher Martin Heidegger called a "dimming down" of the world. Meanwhile our minds, disciplined in the utilitarian ways of science, seek to quiet our amazement at beauty by containing it to a clear cause.

G. K. Chesterton, writing in those early decades after Darwin, scoffed at such a purely utilitarian account of the world. Chesterton took the existence of pleasure, of which beauty is a key part, as one of the ultimate counters to a purely atheistic naturalism. Why does pleasure exist? New life can come by other means. By what absurd logic of survival and reproduction do we get a Bird of Paradise? It is hard to explain these things with any satisfactory answer on the grounds of natural selection alone. Beauty tends to point our vision beyond explanations. Extravagance and excess are simply not necessary on the scale of any biological reality.

Industrial design has recognized, clearly, that more efficiency can be achieved without worrying about ornament. We can build factories without windows more efficiently than with them. Money can be saved by constructing for energy efficiency rather than gaudy extravagance. And yet such places are devoid of meaning. It is beauty that helps make our lives meaningful. The art of replicating and capturing such beauty is a particularly human work.

I won't venture to say what beauty offers to birds in terms of their own lives. But part of what it does for me is give a sense of longing, a desire. When we open ourselves to beauty, we find that it draws us toward the object of our attention, turning that desire toward affection. Beauty has a way of decentering us. As Elaine Scarry points out, simply being in the presence of beauty offers pleasure, whether we possess it or relate to it in any way or not. Put another way, just being close to a hummingbird brings joy. I have no need to own it, to control it, to possess it. Being in its company is all I need, and that presence is something I accept as an extraordinary gift each time it happens. As with the abundance that brings real joy, the pleasure of beauty is based upon participation rather than possession.

We love what is beautiful—that is a human truth reflected through the ages. This reality means that aesthetics, what we judge to be beautiful, is a discipline of great moral weight. Beauty is not simply a matter of taste: I like this and you like that. Beauty is a reality to which we should adjust ourselves, learning over time how to live into its truths. Our notions of beauty will vary between cultures and communities, which is itself a beautifully diverse thing. But beauty is not merely cultural; it comes from a place that is beyond the human. It is, in a way, a reality we receive in whatever container our culture gives us. But receive it we must. Think what you may of hummingbirds, but if you do not find them beautiful, then I think that is a problem in your perception of the world that should be corrected.

July, at least at its beginning, is among the slowest times for birding in Arkansas. The excitement of winter, with its varied vagrants showing up nearly every weekend—wanderers that trigger the local rare bird alerts—has passed. And there is none of the variety and drama of migration until the last days of the month, when shorebirds begin traveling through the state on their journey south. For the most part, July birding is made up of all the familiar residents. But it is just for this reason that it is a good month to really pay attention. This month invites us to turn from the tendency toward acquisition (which so much listing can lead to) and become a contemplative birder instead.

In July, we can dwell with the most common species, still in the full brightness of their breeding plumage, and be in awe.

To truly encounter beauty requires effort, pleasant but arduous. Human beings need contemplation, but our lives rarely allow the attention necessary for it. Harvard art history professor Jennifer Roberts assigns her students the task of going to a museum and sitting before a single piece of art for three hours. These young people find the task akin to torture, at least at first. But with time they begin to see new details, to recognize depth in the images before them that they wouldn't have noticed without such long looking. The *New York Times* worked with Roberts to create a more modest opportunity for attention, asking readers to spend ten minutes with a painting through the *Times* website. A mere 25 percent of those who opened the image were able to stay with it for the allotted time.

Such an inability to stay with a single object might speak to our easily distracted moment, but I think it likely goes deeper than that. It is unusual for us, even in the most natural contexts, to give our attention so fully to one thing. And yet when we do so, we find that our eyes are opened in new ways, our ears attuned to new sounds. It is from this attention, this loving act of presence, that devotion can find its ground.

As I write these words, I'm sitting on a bench in a park not far from my house, surrounded by trees—a mix of oak and pine, a few sugarberries and elm here and there. The birds are raucous with their mid-morning songs. It is a precarious place for a birder to attempt to write. Putting words and thoughts to the page is an act of attention, as is reading them. And yet, despite the birds, I don't feel like they are a distraction. I can look up, I can listen, and yet my words being scrawled across the page are not interrupted. I am in the presence of the world, aware, but not captured by it in the way that a computer screen so often cages my attention. Being here is like reading alongside a good friend, both of us enjoying the books before us, sharing a good line here and there, but always making space for each other's reading.

A Brown Thrasher jumps to the ground in front of me. It is a rusty brown, with heavy streaking across its pale chest. It looks at me with its yellow eye, cocking its head to get a better view before resuming its search for snails amid the leaf litter. A Brown Thrasher is a different kind of bird from a Ruby-throated Hummingbird. It is drab, easily camouflaged. And yet it is beautiful in a simpler way—less gemstone, more Shaker chair.

To appreciate beauty requires a cultivation of taste. We all like this or that, and there are natural bents toward particular forms of beauty, certainly. But there is also a sensitivity toward what is good in things that must be shaped. Part of the work of culture is to help guide our attention to such things. I may not really care for the music of Bach on a first pass. The melodies and harmonies may not appeal to me as much as something on the Top 40 radio channel. But I know that Bach deserves a deeper listen. Like it or not, I need to learn to understand what makes a great work by Bach a piece of music that is both praised and adored, one that has been passed on while so much else has faded.

To see the beauty of a Brown Thrasher can be something like this. It could be judged, so to speak, as an acquired taste. It is a brown, drab, mundane creature on the surface. Its proportions are odd, the yellow of its eye strange, perhaps even uncanny. Why would we call such a bird beautiful?

There is a phrase drawn from Plato's *Republic* that the "good is the beautiful." This gives a moral weight to aesthetics, placing the question of what is beautiful at the heart of the pursuit of goodness. In the first chapter of both the Christian and Jewish Scriptures, it is stated that all things are created and called good. This means that a value has already been given to the world and all that is in it. And if we are to add in Plato's insight, then learning to see the beauty of a bird like a thrasher is to learn to bring our vision in line with our ethics. This bird is good, so we can learn to see the beauty of it. The good is the beautiful.

How we bridge the gap between goodness and beauty for Plato, and many of the Christians who drew on his insights, is through the work of contemplation. When we linger with a thing, when we notice what we might have missed earlier, then we begin to appreciate its subtleties. Plato had a complex theory for how contemplation draws us into the truest nature of things, but we need not adopt his theory to agree with the stance he called us toward. To really embrace the beauty of birds, and so much else in the world, we need to slow down, to sit, and to linger.

Slowness is key here, and we are fortunate to live in a time when many have tasted the fast and found it lacking. We are not alone in our longing for a more patient path. Slow food might be the most famous example of this. When a McDonalds—that embodiment of efficiency over enjoyment—was slated for a historic neighborhood in Rome, Carlo Petrini, an Italian journalist, led a movement against it. What Petrini and those who joined him wanted wasn't food that was fast to get and efficient to eat; they wanted food that was good, full of flavor, and tied to a tradition. From the protest against this McDonalds, the slow food movement began. Since then there have been an array of "slow" movements: slow church, slow cities, and even slow sex. More than just picking up on a trend, these efforts recognize that anything good and pleasurable can easily be turned toward speed and transaction. If we want to savor them in their depths, then sometimes we need to consciously adjust our pace to a different rhythm. It takes culture and the right forms of life and habit to enter that rhythm. And it is a thing that is needed in birding as much as anything else.

In her book *Slow Birding*, Joan Strassmann writes, "All too often, birding is something done racing around in automobiles, stopping for moments to pick up a species here and there, then driving on." Strassmann calls this "motor birding," which is "the birding equivalent to eating fast food." If you've read the chapters that come before this one, you'll see that I am guilty of such fast birding. Sometimes my acquisitive desires push me toward pursuing more species on a list rather than lingering with a particular bird. And yet in a month like July, I am brought back to the common wonders that arrive when I sit still and look. I am rewarded, again and again, by new encounters with neighborhood birds.

Strassmann is an ornithologist, a class of people that she calls the great "slow birders," because the science of ornithology makes one go at a pace of meticulous care. Anyone who has spent time with real researchers will be struck with their profound patience. Some people have dedicated their lives to studying a single species or one small niche in the vast networks of life. How can they do it? Like icons, each object of attention draws them into a world of depth far beyond it. We will never get to the bottom of even a common bird like a cardinal. They will continue to surprise us; attention to their lives will never cease to yield new discoveries. Just as I will never cease to learn new facets of my wife, however many years we've been married, so a researcher will never find out all there is to know about even one aspect of the world around us.

I learned this lesson as a young birder when I attended a meeting of our local Audubon Society chapter. While the topics for discussion were typically bird-related, one month we were going to hear a presentation on the river mussels of Arkansas. I thought such a topic could not possibly fill an hour with anything worth knowing. I was wrong. The talk was the most fascinating I ever heard. Decades later, I can't name more than a couple of the presentations I heard during those years. But because of the loving attention with which the visiting scientist spoke, that mussels presentation stuck.

I've come to see boredom as a moral problem. We get bored not because of some feature of the world but because of a problem in our own attention. The answer to boredom isn't jumping from one thing to the next, like a scroll through a social media feed. It's an offering of ourselves—our time, our looking, our listening—to a quiet world ready to speak.

Like Jennifer Roberts, the Harvard art history professor, Strassmann teaches her students slow birding through assigning them the difficult task of looking. While she was teaching at Rice University in Houston, Texas, Strassmann would ask her students to spend one hour each with Northern Mockingbirds, Great-tailed Grackles, and Yellow-crowned Night Herons, all easily identifiable and readily found species on the Rice campus. The students were to observe the birds carefully, noting how they used time and space, including any differences in how the two sexes behaved (a trick question since male and female Mockingbirds and Night Herons look alike). As with Roberts's art students, these young ornithologists came back with wonder and amazement, all made by slowing down their attention.

It is through this slowness that we often discover beauty. With people, most of us have had the experience of slowly recognizing the beauty of another. There are those who catch our attention immediately, but often we find ourselves drawn to a deeper beauty that isn't so readily visible. Through time spent, attention given, it is as though suddenly a veil is lifted and we recognize a person we've known for a long while as beautiful. In fact, the more time we spend in the presence of someone, the more likely this will be true. And so, too, it is with birds.

I sit on my couch, the afternoon air a heavy mix of heat and humidity. I wish that I could live without air-conditioning, but it is hard to do in an Arkansas July. Out the window, placed beyond a squirrel's jump from the elderberry trees, there is a metal pole with two bird feeders hanging from it. A group of House Finches have settled there, some still downy from the nest. The males are bright with their pink-hued red, and the females are boldly striped with brown like a field of grass, quickly sketched. In the elderberry, a family of Carolina Chickadees arrive. There are three young, the corners of their mouths marked by the wide gapes needed for their feeding. I've watched this happen before, the parents bringing their young on their first visit to a feeder—an important training in the variety of available food in the neighborhood.

Feeding birds was my portal into paying attention to the beauty of birds, and it has continued to be a key feature of my birding life. While I have worked to plant more trees and shrubs, grasses and forbs to support bird life around my yard, I still stock feeders with seed and suet much of the year, as well as sugar-water feeders for the hummingbirds in the summer. Having a bird-feeding station in a yard, or even a single feeder of any kind, can be a good way into the slow kind of birding, which empowers us to see the beauty of birds up close.

I love going into the field, straining my neck to look up at the birds making a life at the tree tops, but the truth is that most field birding is a matter of glimpses—quick looks before the bird is gone. With a feeder, it is easier to wait and watch. I can spend real time with a bird, even getting to know individual visitors over time if I watch closely enough.

Birds certainly fit into categories—family and genus, species and subspecies. But they are also particular individuals. Long looking and careful observation can empower us to see each bird in its particulars. "Beauty always takes place in the particular," writes Scarry, "and if there are no particulars, the chances of seeing it go down." This is the best argument I know for learning to identify birds. Identifying birds is not a means of categorization and control; instead, it is a journey toward the specific, individual reality of each bird. Years ago a friend told me that he liked birds, but he didn't really care to know which species was which. At first I thought this an admirable stance, but I've since come to see something missing in such generalized appreciation. It is important to know, wonder at, and love things in particular.

When we do this with birds, they go from being pretty animals in the general background to being unique creatures. But we should not stop there; they are also, beyond being species, unique individuals. It takes time, and a bird feeder can help, but it is possible to recognize birds at this level. I cannot do so with all the birds in my yard, but I can with some, especially those that have some feature that varies from the standard in some way—a robin with a leucistic white spot on its face, a Blue Jay with an unusual patch of plumage, a pair of Red-tailed Hawks that circle my neighborhood daily.

Such individual variation is another key aspect to beauty. In a review of a book by the evolutionary psychologist Steven Pinker, cultural critic Louis Menand found Pinker's reductionistic views of beauty out of tune with our common experience. Drawing from a study of the statistical average of attractiveness that predicted the most alluring female face, Menand quotes Pinker as saying: "An eye for beauty . . . locks onto faces that show signs of health and fertility—just as one would predict if it had evolved to help the beholder find the fittest mate." Like the Darwinians G. K. Chesterton faulted for not fully appreciating the gratuitousness of pleasure, Pinker sees beauty as nothing more than an evolutionary utility. Menand finds such an argument unsatisfying: "if this were all the eye required the girl in the Pepsodent commercial would be the most desirable woman on earth. And the only person who thinks that is the guy in the Pepsodent commercial. People don't go for faces that deviate from the 'ideal' because they can't have the ideal. They go for them because the deviation is what makes them attractive."

When we slow down our attention to birds, we move from seeing them as a pleasant decoration in the background and begin to see and recognize the lives they have on their own. We see that birds not only carry the characteristics of their species but also the variations and deviations from the "norm" that make them individuals.

In addition to bird feeding, placing nest boxes around our properties can deepen our view into the lives of birds. One of the great scientists of bird behavior, Bernd Heinrich, took this opportunity for close observation to the next level when he discovered a pair of Northern Flickers setting up a nest in the exterior wall of his rural cabin. Rather than chase the birds off, Heinrich created an opening on the interior so that he could watch what was happening in the nest. Most of us won't go to those lengths to see a bird's life cycle so up close, but just watching a nest box from afar is an experience of wonder. And while they can have their problems, there are a number of camera-equipped nest boxes on the market that can give you an unobtrusive view into the secrets of bird homelife.

Why do we want to see inside a nest box, to know an individual bird, to go ever deeper into our experience of birds in their particular, individual lives? In his book *Why Literature Still Matters*, professor of classics Jason M. Baxter writes of an experience he had while trying to see a remote seaside vista on an Italian island. This ocean view was not accessible by road or boat, but only by a long hike through an arid landscape with poorly marked trails. Baxter, in making his way to the view, found that he was lost, and his supply of water quickly ran out. When he finally got to the vista, he was desperate for water and cut and bruised from the hike. And yet his experience of the vista was one of profound beauty. Once he was able to get more water and find his way home again, he had the desire to do it all again.

In seeking to understand this experience, Baxter draws on an insight from C. S. Lewis's essay *The Weight of Glory*, writing that "when we encounter beauty, it is almost always accompanied by a strange note of sorrow, a sorrow that arises because beauty feels like something *over there*, something external to me." When he comes across something beautiful, Baxter says, "what I find myself wanting is not just to *see* beauty, but to *be* beauty, to make that which I see (or hear or read) become a permanent part of my being." By arriving at the seaside vista dehydrated and bruised, Baxter had in some way entered the frame of the beautiful. He was looking at it, but the journey had also made him a part of it.

I think Baxter's explanation works to describe our experience with birds as well. In our watching, our listening, there is a love. But it is often one-sided. We stand apart, mere observers. We want not merely to *see* the beauty of wild creatures but to *be* a part of it.

And yet the truth is that we *are* a part of it. Each of us is a part of the wild world that we watch through our windows, whose beauty we observe through our binoculars. We are not birds, but we are creatures the birds have long known. What we need to do is to reclaim some of that deep wild relationship we have with these creatures. We need to reclaim wildness within ourselves. It requires work, a breaking out of our self-enclosed zoos, but watching wild creatures can help us begin to bend the bars.

In the documentary *My Octopus Teacher*, South African filmmaker Craig Foster goes for daily dives in the great African Kelp Forest near his home. He leaves behind tanks and a wetsuit, opting to dive with as little equipment as possible so that he can learn to feel this underwater forest in its fullness. Over time, as the film traces, Foster begins a relationship with a particular octopus. From her, he learns not only about her and her kind but about life in the ocean and his place in it.

Following the success of the film, Foster wrote a book called *Amphibious Soul.* It is the story of his desire to reclaim his own wildness. In reading the book, you realize that though Foster's relationship with the octopus was unique, it was not a one-off experience. Foster recounts many times of profound, close encounters with wild creatures, often with species that are quite elusive. Reflecting on these encounters in conversation with Indigenous trackers, Foster writes that Indigenous people "understand that this is the pattern of life: that nature is alive and intelligent and reciprocal, and that the animals we seek to know sometimes seem to be looking back at us."

One morning, before the heat began its rising blaze on the graph of my weather app, I went for a hike in a local woodland park. I go there several times a week, and in some seasons daily. I know all its trails and many of its creatures. Walking quietly along a side trail that is not often traveled, I noticed a bird above me. It was a Tufted Titmouse, a small gray bird with pinkish sides and a crest like a cardinal. They have deep black eyes, and this titmouse had hers trained on me.

Aware that I was being watched, I stopped. The titmouse hopped down the branches of the trees above, like a spiral staircase, coming closer and closer to me, until she was on the branch directly over my head. I could see the soft down of her feathers, the beautiful subtle colors of her sides. She leaned down over the side of the branch and looked directly at me for what felt like ten minutes. It was likely only a few seconds. Still, in that moment, there was recognition, a mutual looking.

It took slowness to create an opening for it to happen—quiet, attentive looking on both our parts. In that encounter we were together, two creatures acknowledging one another, and it was beautiful.

8

AUGUST

Naming

THE AIRPORT HUMMED with the low rumble of engines as I turned past the northeast runway. Kingbirds, both Eastern and Western, along with their *Tyrannus* cousins, Scissor-tailed Flycatchers, bobbed up and down from the barbed wire barrier on the chain-link fence around the landing areas. The pavement of the perimeter road was smooth, a shimmering heat radiating from the blacktop. I could feel it in my face, my back sweating along the contours of my backpack.

My feet moved in circles, pushing and pulling, as my bicycle stayed steady at a speed just below 20 mph. I glanced left, down toward a swampy spot by the river, searching for a sign of an elusive Black-crowned Night Heron I see sometimes, hiding along the brushy edge of a pond.

There had been a report of a Piping Plover at the River Port, an industrial park where a muddy field often attracts migrating shorebirds. In August, when the heat hangs heavy, shorebirds are the lure that draws birders back out from the air-conditioning that kept many inside for most of July. I was trying to see as many birds by bike as I could, as well as training for a century bike ride in September. So riding the ten miles to the River Port by bicycle was a way to both get in some training and tally up birds in one excursion.

As I rode, I thought about what else might be at the Port. There would be Killdeer, a black-banded plover that is perhaps the most common shorebird of the area. Greater and Lesser Yellowlegs, appropriately named species with long, bright yellow legs, would be likely. Least Sandpipers, the smallest of what birders call the "peeps" for their small size and the sound of their calls, would be in the mix this time of year. Semipalmated Sandpipers, named for the "palmated" webs of skin between their toes, would be strong possibilities. Their close relative, the Western Sandpiper, would also be a rare possibility, as would a Baird's Sandpiper, the largest of the "peeps." The Baird's Sandpiper was named by the ornithologist Elliott Coues for his mentor Spencer Fullerton Baird, the second secretary of the Smithsonian Institution. Going through such a list of bird names, you get everything from descriptions of clear physical features, to references to geography, to the history of ornithological documentation.

The names of these birds, of course, are their common ones. All birds also have a Latin, scientific name, bearing the signature "binomial nomenclature" of Linnaeus—genus and species. In some parts of the world, especially many Latin American countries, the scientific names are generally used by all. But most English-speaking birders refer to the birds by their common names. Because the common names are so prevalent, they are agreed upon and standardized by ornithological authorities like the American Ornithological Society. Many, like my grandfather call Northern Cardinals "red birds," and there are a variety of regional variations for many common species. But the official common names birders use are set. Such standardization, like uniform spelling, ensures everyone means the same thing when recording observations. It also helps keep everyone on the same page as taxonomies shift.

Taxonomy is the science of naming and classifying organisms. How does this species relate to that one? How does this family of birds differ from that family? These are the kinds of questions taxonomists work through, balancing a variety of sources of information, from genetic studies to field observations. To be a birder for any length of time is to learn flexibility with names. Over my birding life I've had to relearn dozens of bird names, largely because species were either lumped or split. When species are lumped, two groups of birds that were considered distinct species are reclassified as one species. For instance, the small flycatchers that were called Pacific-slope and Cordilleran were lumped in recent years into a single species: the Western Flycatcher. Birders hate these lumps, because if you had both on your life list, you lose a species overnight.

Splits go the opposite direction. For instance, the common Rufous-sided Towhee was split into the Spotted Towhee (more prevalent in the western part of the United States) and the Eastern Towhee (more abundant in the east). In both cases, the ornithological winds could change. As birders who have been keeping lists for decades know, the same bird can jump back and forth, on and off a list according to the latest taxonomic trends. The Western Flycatcher, after all, was split into two distinct species in 1989 . . . only to be lumped again in 2023.

It is all part of the dynamic science of understanding what a species is, which is also a question of art and philosophy. Because naming in not only a matter of science but of identity.

In the Hebrew Bible, the first task given to a human being is to name the animals. This is a significant act. Names create relationship; they foster meaning. But they can also be a form of control. Look, for instance, at the history of a certain mountain in Alaska. Denali is the name that was given the mountain by the Koyukon people who had been the residents of the area for centuries. But then a gold prospector named the mountain after William McKinley, the then-candidate for and soon-to-be president of the United States. From 1917 to 2015 that name remained, until the US Department of the Interior officially accepted the traditional native name for the peak. Then, after his inauguration in 2025, one of Donald Trump's first executive actions was to change the name back to Mount McKinley.

This back and forth, to name and rename a mountain, shows how much power what we call something can have. This was one of Trump's first actions upon returning to office for his second term. It was a symbolic action that, along with a changing of the name of the Gulf of Mexico to the Gulf of America, echoed his agenda. And of course, officially adopting the name Denali for the mountain in 2015 was also an act of political significance. Names are necessary; they are how we communicate about the world around us. But they also shape that world. Names form the relationships we have with people and places, with creatures and ourselves.

What we name things, and how we name them, is a question with deep implications for how we live in the world.

I followed the road around the airport through the harrowing entrance and exit of the main terminal. Pushing hard, I increased my speed to match the cars as best I could and get beyond the airport as quickly as possible. I turned south, following the blacktop of Lindsey Road past Remmel Park. I had a brief respite from the heat as I passed beneath the interstate bridge, emerging again as the road curved past a Circle K convenience store. Scissor-tailed Flycatchers flew from the power lines as I pedaled, their long tails bobbing in the humid air.

My friend Ariana Remmel is related to the Remmel for whom the park is named, Pratt Remmel, a former mayor of our city. Ariana is a science journalist, and they wrote an important story for *Audubon* magazine on the question of names, especially names like that for the park and road—honorifics. More than a hundred North American common bird names are honorifics—birds like the Baird's Sandpiper—named after a friend or mentor of the person who first described it for science. When the bird is named after the person themselves, they are called eponyms. Either way, most of these names were applied in the mid-nineteenth century, a time of US expansion and colonial ambition. As the health and wealth gospel preachers say, "name it and claim it" was the impulse of the time.

The power to name is the power to control. From ancient times, names have represented an encapsulation of the essence of a place, a person, or a creature. In the Christian Gospels, Jesus never allows the demons to say his name, but he often wants to know theirs. Naming is an act of power, for good or for ill.

The colonialists, be they part of government or the academy, sought to rename the world according to their kind. It was a way of establishing power. In recent years people have recognized and questioned that impulse. Many in the birding community have noted that those honored with a bird name weren't all that honorable. From grave robbers to slaveholders, Confederate generals to white supremacists, those honored in our field guides and bird lists were people we would not want our children to emulate.

In 2020, birders Jordan Rutter and Gabriel Foley began an online campaign to push against the use of honorifics and eponyms. They called their effort "Bird Names for Birds." Their agenda was simple and straightforward: rename birds based on features that actually relate to birds themselves rather than to people.

While many honorifics are benign, if not helpful, many are deeply hurtful to birders whose ancestors suffered under projects of colonialism. Cherokee birder Stephen Carr Hampton writes about why "Scott's Oriole" is the most problematic bird name for him. The bird was named for General Winfield Scott, the very officer who oversaw the horrors of Cherokee removal from Georgia, inaugurating the Trail of Tears. The oriole was named in Scott's honor by another army officer, Darius Couch, whose name is attached to the Couch's Kingbird. These bird names, though a part of a certain history, are not a means of preserving it. Instead, as Hampton and others show, they are signs of the erasure of people and names we may never recover.

In their article, Ariana Remmel talks with ornithologist J. Drew Lanham, a Black writer and professor whose book *The Home Place* is one of the best expressions of ecological belonging. Lanham lives in South Carolina, at the heart of the range of a bird now called the Bachman's Sparrow, a species bearing the name John James Audubon gave in honor of his friend John Bachman. Bachman was a Lutheran minister from South Carolina who enslaved people and was among the most prominent clergy defending the institution of slavery. Bachman wrote essays arguing that Black people were intellectually inferior and thus could be enslaved without moral hazard to the enslaver. He, like many others, is clearly not someone we would choose to honor.

White supremacy is reason enough to remove someone's name from a bird. The power of the Bird Names for Birds campaign, however, goes deeper than simply making a moral inventory of those undeserving of honor. As its name implies, Bird Names for Birds is a call to end the practice of honorifics and eponyms altogether. Rather than being the moral arbiters of what they call "verbal statues," names that stand like confederate monuments, the campaign organizers call instead for a commonsense adoption of names that help us understand the bird we are naming. Greater Yellowlegs tells you something about what bird we might encounter on a mudflat. Even poetic names like Mourning Dove describe the somber song we might hear on a hot afternoon. If we give names that help us understand something about the bird, then we are helped in relating to the species. Naming isn't just about a claim of possession; it can be a way of facilitating relationship. Bird Names for Birds seeks to do just that.

Lanham, for instance, chooses to call the Bachman's Sparrows that live in the pine forests of his native South Carolina, Pinewoods Sparrows. Like the Pine Warbler, the name tells you quite a lot about what kind of species this bird really is. I've never seen a ~~Bachman's~~ Pinewoods Sparrow away from a pine forest—that's where they're found—so why not offer us that clue in the name itself? "We're limiting birds to the fallibility of humanity," Lanham is quoted as saying in the article, "and that is a way of owning what should be wild and free from the names of humans that hang on their backs."

The Bird Names for Birds efforts have been successful. The American Ornithological Society, a normally slow-to-move organization, decided in 2023 that it will do away with honorifics and eponyms for all English common names for birds. This was a major step, one that will mean that many bird names in this very book will end up changing in time. The process will likely be slow, but in the end, I hope, it will empower birders to engage with the species around them in a fuller way, a way that enables them to relate to the birds around them and learn their stories.

After following the road past a factory that prints highway signs and a wide space where a windmill-blade manufacturer had been replaced by a steel mill, I came to the open space where water was pooled beside a muddy edge. This land is the area where construction rubble is being used to fill in the wetland, a field that will one day be an industrial site like all the others. I have never once seen it dry. Even on an August day like this one, after weeks without rain, water from the river somehow makes its way to the field, along with the crustaceans and fish that swim in the deeper channels. This water, with its mud, small fish, and large crawfish, makes an excellent place for birds migrating through the area. And the elevated road running around it makes for a good place to watch them.

As I came closer to the wet field, I could see birds of various shapes and sizes bobbing and feeding at the water's edge. I pulled my binoculars from the pouch strapped to my handlebars and began scanning. On this side, there were mostly Killdeer, a strangely named bird whose origins is obscured by history. Most likely the name, like a chickadee's, simply comes from its loud call which could be interpreted as ***kill-deer, kill-deer***. It is not a sound birders, especially photographers, like to hear. As Pete Dunne writes of the Killdeer's call in *The Shorebirds of North America*, "This loud alarm call is a signal for other shorebirds to disperse, since danger may be right around the corner." Thankfully, these Killdeer were busy picking insects from the mud and weren't issuing their alarm.

In trying to prevent the loss of this wetland, I contacted the US Army Corps of Engineers, the agency responsible for permitting the infill of wetlands under the Clean Water Act. When they sent me their permitting documents, I saw that the land I was now looking at had been classified as "dry land." This determination was made, as the permit said, from a desk with no visit to the site. Because the land was called a "dry uplands," it was not granted the protection a wetland connected to the river would require. This designation was clearly a bureaucratic lie, but when I pressed the Army Corps on it, they responded coldly that I was free to file a Freedom of Information Act request. It was a laborious hurdle that I chose to forgo, given that our group of birders was making progress with constructive rather than confrontational approaches with the Port Authority. Still, the language of such land classification shows the problem and power naming can have for how we treat the world.

There is a theory in philosophy and linguistics called the Sapir–Whorf Hypothesis. It originated with Edward Sapir, an anthropologist who did groundbreaking work with the Hopi Indians, and Benjamin Lee Whorf, one of Sapir's students, whose papers helped lead to new theories of how language shapes our perception of reality. Whorf originally trained in chemistry and worked as a fire prevention specialist. In that work, he once encountered a factory where drums of highly flammable chemicals were stored. In one area of the factory, these drums were labeled "full," and the workers treated them with appropriate caution, being sure not to smoke near them. In another area, the drums that had been emptied were labeled accordingly, though they still contained flammable chemicals. Whorf noticed that though the workers knew that these drums were still a fire hazard, they treated them carelessly, including smoking near them—all because of how the label of "empty" formed their perceptions.

Whorf died of cancer at the age of forty-four, but his teacher Edward Sapir helped publish his collected papers that would lead to what came to be called the Sapir–Whorf Hypothesis. The theory's most basic idea is that language forms our perceptions of reality and helps explain why naming is so important. Dry land or wetland: These names matter not only legally but in our way of relating to a place. Call a field a wetland and it is given protections and legal weight. Call it dry, and you can do what you want.

Writers know the power of names. Essayist and novelist Marilynne Robinson, in her essay "Surrendering Wilderness," writes that "wilderness is where things can be done that would be intolerable in a populous landscape." Speaking especially of placing nuclear waste in the "wilderness" of Utah, Robinson names the fact that so often we hold on to wilderness as a way of excusing what we do in our working landscapes. Wilderness is not only a place where we get away from civilization but also a place where we hide its effects. Because of this, Robinson writes that "we must surrender the idea of wilderness, accept the fact that the consequences of human presence in the world are universal and ineluctable."

Whether it is a question of honorifics or properly naming a landscape, what we call something is a matter of moral weight. It can help or hinder our way toward knowing the world and relating to it, either as a means of exploitation and extraction or as a place of mutuality and affection.

As I scanned the mudflats, I noticed a car parked on the other side of the field, with a man standing beside it with a tripod and spotting scope. Another birder! I biked around the field to the other side to meet him. When I pulled up, binoculars around my neck, I started with the important questions first: Have you seen the Piping Plover? Yes, it's right over there, he pointed, indicating a muddy spot at the eastern edge of the field before us. I looked through my binoculars and there it was: a plover that looks similar to a Killdeer, yet with a single band on its chest as opposed to the Killdeer's double band. It also had a bright orange bill and legs and a light gray back, all marks that distinguished it from the more common migrating plover, the Semipalmated. Once I'd had a good look at the bird, I introduced myself to the birder. We'd never met in person but knew each other's names, both of us finding unusual birds often enough that we show up on the rare bird alert listings. Roger was his name, and he'd retired to the area after having lived other places around the country—including Chicago, where a group of Piping Plovers nest on the shore of Lake Michigan. I'd lived there as well, and we talked about the plovers and the other birds on the mudflats before us, connected to geographies both personal and distant.

With each bird's name, a story began to emerge. We couldn't know for sure, but it was likely that this Piping Plover was one of those that nested on the shores of the Great Lakes. Nearby was a White-rumped Sandpiper that had likely, just a few weeks ago, been in the Arctic Circle. Beside it was a Greater Yellowlegs that had nested in the lower latitudes of Canada. By knowing each bird's name, we could begin to know something of their place in the larger dance of life, their habits and relationships.

As a priest, I am often called to assist with funerals for people I did not know—a friend or family member of someone in the church, a person who has spent the last decade disconnected from the church but still considers my congregation their community of faith. Birth, marriage, death—church is where even many otherwise secular people turn to mark the sacred.

In meeting with the family before the funeral, or when a friend speaks at the wake, there is a moment when the story of the person is told. It is in that story that we gain a sense of who they were and what we have lost in their passing—the unique life of each person. Whether I knew the person or not, I always leave with a sense of the unique wonder each of us is, and how it is often by the smallest gestures that we create significance.

In her work on ecological grief, the theologian Hannah Malcolm calls for a renewal of the work of naming. Recognizing the myriad problems of naming, she writes that "The act of naming . . . ought not to be an abstract exercise, nor a detached articulation of power, but a loving response." We practice this response, Malcolm writes, when we "learn the names of creatures, landscape features, people, and places, and . . . pass those names on in our speech. This helps us attend to our environment in a way that deepens our sense of belonging to it." By learning these names and using them, we "strengthen our love for the world."

As a priest, Malcolm sees a key role for this naming in the work of prayer. Christian prayers have long included the names of those we are bringing before God as a community. In the liturgy of the Book of Common Prayer, there are often places to name aloud those who are suffering and those who have died, as well as both civil and church leaders. In each case, we use the person's first name, for prayer is always an intimate and personal act. By together naming those we grieve and the needs our community bears, we are able to see "a place as it really is."

A name, as we've mentioned, is a door, an entrance into which we are invited to see a whole story, the story of a species and a life. Most birders' personal libraries begin with field guides—illustrated books with images and names. The first task of a birder is to learn which bird is which. But as a birder grows, they go beyond reading general guides and begin turning toward life histories—the specific stories of individual bird lives—as well as other books that deepen their understanding of birds. In *What It's Like to Be a Bird*, for instance, David Sibley, whose field guides appear in most birders' libraries, goes deeper to explore the lives of birds in a way that moves us toward sympathy. Through deep description of various birds' ways of living, we are invited to imaginatively enter their world.

Sibley's friend and regular collaborator, Pete Dunne, has a brilliant way of opening our eyes to the lives of birds without collapsing their otherness into mere human terms. His book *The Courage of Birds* names a virtue that birds exhibit in their work to survive the bitter cold of northern winters. And in *The Wind Masters*, he tells the stories of North American birds of prey, but with a desire to understand what it might be like to live as those birds rather than simply recounting the biological facts. Jennifer Ackerman's books, such as *The Genius of Birds*, expand our range of appreciation by mixing science and storytelling to help us appreciate the intelligence of birds. And species-specific books like *Crow Planet* by Lyanda Lynn Haupt tells the story of a specific group of birds.

In recent years, the Birds of the World website has offered an immense resource that gives detailed information on nearly every known species of bird on the globe. It is a regular resource I turn to when I see a new species or realize that I have no idea where some common winter resident, such as the Winter Wrens that visit my local woodland park, spend their summers. In their case, and another example of the perils of naming, Winter Wrens summer in Canada and some of the Great Lakes' states, where they are not seen in winter. "Summer Wren?" Perhaps our names should be relative. This is the case with the birds North Americans know as warblers for their melodious songs. In Latin America these birds are called "los chipes," because they do not sing on their wintering grounds, but only make *chip* notes. The Magnolia Warblers that move through my neighborhood, singing in April, are known in Mexico as Chipe de Magnolia.

Names vary by context, and with these shifting names, our possibility for relationship is broadened, like people who know us both professionally and casually. Birders who get the chance to see Magnolia Warblers both on their nesting grounds and Chipes de Magnolia on their wintering grounds are thrilled to have a window into the complex, globe-trotting, name-shifting lives of these small birds.

After half an hour scanning the mudflat, I had found, named, and recorded all that I could see or hear. The day was getting hot, and I still had a ten-mile bike ride ahead of me to get back home. I packed my binoculars in the case on my handlebars and pulled on the backpack that held my scope. As I rode west, Eurasian Collared Doves made their crow-like caws as they flew from the power lines, and Western

Kingbirds dipped over the mown fields of the Port. Just before I came to the gas station, I passed a place that held the memory of one of my best birding moments.

My family appreciates my birding, but my wife and daughters don't have the same drive to go into the field as I do. However, just before the pandemic, they gave me a board game called Wingspan, which they now happily play with me. In the game, players work with various bird cards, each featuring a species. The object is to populate your game board habitats—forest, grassland, and wetland—with as many high-value bird species as possible, while accruing additional points for eggs, food cached, and various other point-scoring opportunities. Through the game, my family was given some sense of what made the birds I love so special, as they were able to see them illustrated up close, in a format that held their attention. We played the game a good deal in the first spring of the pandemic, when we couldn't get together with other people.

Then, one evening, my family agreed to accompany me to the Port for a short birding trip. We saw the Western Kingbirds that nest in the Port each summer, one of the farthest eastern parts of its range, and everyone was wowed by the extravagant beauty of the Scissor-tailed Flycatchers that also summer in the grassy, open fields of the area.

As we were beginning to make our way back, my youngest daughter called out, "Wait, what was that bird?" My wife had seen the same bird on the wire, and offered, "Oh, I think it was just a Mourning Dove." Wanting to honor my daughter's question and knowing that often the best birds come as a flash on the roadside, I stopped the car, and we got out to investigate.

It turned out that the dove my daughter had seen was a White-winged Dove, a bird that is relatively rare for Arkansas. The dove sat preening, and I was able to get my spotting scope set up on it so that everyone could get a good look.

From playing the game to recognizing when something was different about a dove, my family was beginning to engage in the work of noticing the particular, unique lives of birds. This work was made possible by learning their names and something of their stories. We know that when we learn our human neighbors' names and stories, we form a bond and spark community. To learn the name and story of a person is a path toward affection and care—or at least a humane and common decency.

But our neighborhoods, the rippling circles of our influence, are not confined to the human. We have wild neighbors too, and they share our lives more than we think. A building project to create jobs for humans could mean the disappearance of a critical migratory stop for birds. It is easy to think only of the building project when you don't know the story of the birds. But when you begin to know the story, then the actions we take become more complicated.

As I rode home past factories and around the airport, the summer air heavy with ground-level ozone, the result of heat and car exhaust, I couldn't help but feel the heaviness of human life upon the planet. It is easy to be discouraged as even marginal habitats, like the small wetland at the Port, are covered over by the insatiable beat of the economy. Still, part of what gives me hope are the names I know, the names that represent a community continuing life. And as I teach my daughters those names, I hope that some of them will spark a relationship and, with it, care.

In Hannah Malcolm's talk she brought in the work of the French philosopher Jean-Louis Chrétien, who writes of naming as an "Ark of Speech." I like that idea, for it gives greater meaning to the work with which I've long been involved, the work of knowing the names of birds. Perhaps, in some way, by looking across a muddy, marginal field and saying, "There's a Piping Plover," "There are two Greater Yellowlegs and ten Killdeer," "There's a White-rumped Sandpiper," I am creating a life raft on which they can grab hold and survive. To say their names, I am saying, "Here are more than a bunch of birds." These are creatures with lives and stories who are making an incredible journey. It would be decent of us to stop our constant push for more, our demand for "growth," and let them have a resting place.

9

SEPTEMBER

Vision

I WOKE IN the musty warmth of the old hotel, beautiful and charming but with no air-conditioning or expansive rooms. Walking around the king-sized bed shoved in a space meant for smaller mattresses, I tried to dress without waking Emily. More importantly, I started the anti-nausea routine that had accompanied the pre-trip instructions—a mix of proper hydration and a good dose of Dramamine. I took it to heart, having learned on a deep-sea fishing trip years ago that I am most certainly a landlubber. For all the amazing sightings of giant sea turtles, my visits to the bow had dimmed the day's joy.

Chewing on ginger gum, I walked from the hotel and down the tree-lined Alvarado Street. It was mostly dark, a hint of light just beginning in the east, a hazy mix of the rising sun with the halogen streetlamps glowing in the morning fog. I saw no one on the sidewalks or road as I found my way to the Monterey pier. In the maze of boats, I wondered whether I was walking in the right direction, but once on the boardwalk, I saw a couple with binoculars heading in the same direction.

The sea lions were beginning their noisy barks, and the gulls were joining in the raucous seaside song as I caught up with the couple. The husband had on an eBird hat and quickly told me that this was their second trip with Shearwater in two days. "I have a hard time finding new life birds," he bragged, indicating a life list likely in the seven hundred species range for the American Bird Association (ABA) Area, a region that spans the United States and Canada, including Hawaii. Not feeling too sorry for him, I followed as we walked the plank onto the waiting boat. If someone with a list like that could expect new birds on this trip, I could hope for dozens, having never birded beyond the shoreline and barely at all on the West Coast.

Birds, more than any other class of animals, have found niches in every place on earth. From pole to pole, continent to continent, these feathered creatures live in every imaginable habitat. And given that the earth is mostly ocean, birds have also found ways to live in its vast expanses, playing key roles in its cycles of life.

A variety of birds—from the robin-sized storm petrels to the massive, long-winged albatrosses—spend most of their lives far out at sea. These pelagic birds travel far and wide, weathering storms, surviving sharks, and coming to land only when nesting demands it. Heading into the bay, I was about to be introduced to a whole world of birds I'd never encountered.

Once the group had gathered on the boat—a couple dozen of us from across the world, it seemed—Debi Shearwater introduced herself. Having changed her last name to match a prominent family of ocean birds, Debi is a legend of pelagic birding. Known for suffering no fools, she has been the queen of West Coast pelagic birding for decades, with a long list of bird records to her name. Beginning in an era when women were not at the forefront of birding, she became the go-to guide for Monterey Bay and worked actively to empower women in the male-dominated world of serious birding. There was even a character loosely based on her in the film *The Big Year*: a pelagic guide named Annie Auklet, portrayed by Angelica Huston.

Now Debi had announced her retirement, and this would be her last season leading regular pelagic tours in Monterey Bay. In a lucky turn, thanks to someone else's cancellation, I'd been able to snag a seat on a September tour, right at the peak of seabird season. As it happened, this trip also fell on Debi Shearwater's birthday. The mix of it all made me feel like I was participating in a day of birding history even before we left the dock.

As a teenager first learning about the world of birding, I'd been introduced to Shearwater through Pete Dunne's book *The Feather Quest*. The book chronicles Dunne's North American "Big Year": an attempt to see as many birds as possible in a calendar year. Reading it taught me about America's greatest birding hotspots and birders, as well as infecting me with a long-running desire for Zeiss binoculars—the thing my teenage desires turned toward far more than any sports car. Writing of Shearwater's pre-trip spiel, Dunne said: "Pelagic birding has a cult quality, and Debi's litany on the bow, spoken forty-five times a year, goes off with the seductive sameness of *Rocky Horror*."

Now I was here, listening for the first time to that spiel. It was, for a birder, like getting to see the cult classic for its last run. Debi, it was clear, loves Monterey Bay and wanted us to know just how significant a place it is. "The bay is as vast and unique a place as the Grand Canyon," she said, "with life as varied as the African Savannah. We just don't see most of it because it's underwater." What we *would* see were the birds and mammals that have come to participate in that great swirl of life, bound in their different ways to the oxygen-rich surface.

Debi then turned to the topic of birding. People who go on tours like this are not usually casual about their pursuits. To spend the money and risk a day of seasickness for the sake of seeing a life bird is not for the faint of heart. Looking around the crowd, I saw nothing but that triumvirate of elite binocular brands—Swarovski, Leica, and my beloved Zeiss. And yet Debbie cautioned this experienced and serious birding set: "if this is your first pelagic birding trip, don't get frustrated at not being able to catch sight of the birds or identify them." She went on to explain that however good you are with warblers in the trees, sparrows in a meadow, or shorebirds on a mudflat, watching birds in the vast expanse of ocean waves is completely different.

"To see birds out there," she said with an air of initiating us into occult knowledge, "you'll need to retrain your vision."

Vision is different from sight. To see is to pick up on light and shade, color and motion, distance and stillness. A camera can see; it can gather the data and turn it into a record of a moment's light. A computer also can see, reading the data of a particular scene. But neither a camera nor a computer can have vision, for vision is seeing with meaning. Vision is the ability to resolve a flash of movement against the dark waves and call it a storm petrel. Vision is the power to bring the senses into conversation with both knowledge and imagination so that the fragments of sight can be made whole.

Wendell Berry, in his book *Imagination in Place*, writes that this truth is why he writes about his place, the rural community of Port Royal, Kentucky, through the fictional town of Port William, Kentucky. He writes beautiful poetry and piercing essays, but it is through fiction that he reflects the full story of the rural Kentucky community in which he has lived most of his life. "Works of imagination come of an impulse to transcend the limits of experience or provable knowledge in order to make a thing that is whole," writes Berry. "What one actually or probably knows about an actual experience is never complete; it cannot, within the limits of memory or factual records, be made whole. Imagination 'completes the picture' by transcending the actual memories and provable facts."

We often think of imagination as pure fantasy, or making things up. But it is a necessary part of any human work of observation. Imagination is, literally, an "imaging." We think of scientists as people who live with the most exacting observations of pure sight. But those scientists who have expanded our understanding of the world most profoundly rely heavily on imagination to actually "see" the world beyond our senses. Who can see a quark? By what measure can we observe time? To sense them in their wholeness takes an act of imagination.

Birding, to turn from sight to vision, needs imagination as well. This doesn't mean that birders make up what they see. But in my experience, those birders with the most imagination for what is possible tend to find it actualized. This isn't some form of manifesting; it is instead the path to truly seeing what we would otherwise miss. Most birders, for instance, would go to the Lake Dardanelle Dam and see hundreds of Ring-billed Gulls and leave it at that. Kenny Nichols, however, looks at that swirling mass of white and wonders if a Short-billed Gull might be among them. Kenny is an excellent observer and has the ability of any good birder: to clue in on anything different in a large flock. But I doubt he would be able to find as many rare birds as he has if he didn't have some imagination for what was possible.

As we pulled out of the harbor, cormorants were gathered among the sea lions and a scattering of seals. We scanned the rocky shore. "Black Oystercatcher!" someone cried out, and all gathered to see the shorebird, a West Coast exclusive with a long orange bill, picking mollusks from the rocks.

Everyone was free to call a bird when they saw it, but Shearwater had a couple of "spotters" working with her—skilled birders who would point out species along the way. There is a certain skill in both pointing out birds and in following someone else's instructions for finding them. Both take practice. There's a fast shorthand for directions that requires a decent knowledge of the face of a clock. "There, midway up the black rocks, at three o'clock," someone might call. Here, too, an act of imagination is required—the ability to overlay a clock face on the visual field in front of you. You must rely on imagination to follow the metaphors of language and tame the chaotic field of data. For birding in the open ocean, points of common reference are harder to come by. For this reason, the boat itself becomes the orienting object. As Dunne recounts Debi's instructions on his trip, "The bow (pointy end of most boats) is twelve o'clock; the stern (the other end) is six o'clock. All the other numbers fall (regular as clockwork) in between."

According to the philosopher Charles Taylor, it is this ability to paint pictures with language that makes us human. We are not simply creatures who can accurately describe our environments in ever more precise ways. Instead, human beings can create whole new modes of vision through language and shared attention. What we create through language can "reveal what is there, and reconnect us with it."

Even if birders don't always know it, we do this essentially human work all the time. We act like poets who help name the otherwise unseen world around us, creating it together through our naming and description. To see a species is to see something that a human being noticed and differentiated, a creature that was then named. Species names are always shifting, as we have seen, and there are bases for these changes in genetics, patterns of interbreeding, and redressing the wrongs of the past.

But in the end, names are imagined things we agree to use. They are constructs that help us interpret the world, to know where to look when someone says, "Pink-footed Shearwater, two o'clock!"

The boat moved into deeper waters. As we traveled away from the shore, we watched sea otters gathered in a bed of kelp, playfully rolling and diving, floating on their backs as they worked to free meat from the shells of oysters and urchins. The farther out we went, the more the sense of space became strange and disorienting. The landmarks of shore were gone, and we were surrounded by nothing but water in all directions.

Soon, though, the life on the surface began to mark the contours of the world below us. Humpback whales emerged, spraying water and leaping with their impossible bodies from the sea. It was like a nature documentary brought to salt-spraying vividness. The whales were drawn by masses of plankton, and wherever the whales were, a swirl of creatures accompanied them, terns and gulls and shearwaters, feeding from all the life the whales stirred up from the deep.

Most birds have excellent vision. They can see more colors than humans do, and often at farther distances. For instance, most birds are able to see the ultraviolet spectrums that are invisible to human perception. Ocean birds also have red and yellow oils in their eyes that help them see in hazy conditions. And of course birds rely on sound to communicate. But it was long thought that birds can't smell, or if they did, it wasn't among their greatest powers. In recent years, however, ornithologists have begun to demonstrate that a wide range of birds *can* smell. Some can even map whole landscapes according to scent. Chief among these are seabirds, who, more than any other birds, are often forced to navigate without any visual inputs. Researchers at Oxford University have demonstrated that seabirds can navigate by scent.

This sense of smell is not just for navigation. Seabirds can tell, from great distances, where the fish are. That's why many birding groups use chumming—releasing putrid fish scraps and oils across the water behind the boat. It's like hanging a bird feeder on the ocean, and the birds of these waters, accustomed to a quickly changing buffet, come in quickly. As we moved out, Debbie called for chum to be dropped, and soon after, the birds gathered off the boat's wake, twisting and diving after the scraps of seafood.

In his book *Scientific Realism and the Plasticity of Mind*, the philosopher Paul Churchland offers a helpful insight into the work of vision. Following philosophers from Immanuel Kant to Thomas Kuhn, Churchland accepts the idea that our "perceptual judgments must be laden with theory." In looking, we don't see the world as it is, in itself. Rather, we filter it through our understandings and categories. This doesn't mean that there isn't a real world or even that our perceptions are wrong; it simply means that our perceptions of the world aren't just a simple act of letting in the light of raw-sense data. We aren't cameras; we're conscious actors in the work of understanding the world.

Sometimes, however, our understandings and our perceptions become mismatched. For instance, most people understand that the earth rotates as it travels around the sun. And yet we still *sense* that it is the sun going around the earth. Churchland proposed that we should fix this problem by changing our perceptions through training. Given its plasticity, the brain can be reshaped, as can our perceptions. It would be better for us, Churchland proposes, to see the world as we know it to be through our best theories rather than how it *seems*. We should seek to mold our minds to reflect the latest and best science.

As an example of the sort of rewiring Churchland proposes, think about getting up in the morning and watching the sun rise. As you do, remember that the sun is a fixed object relative to our moving planet. To practice this perception, imagine that you are standing at the top of a down escalator in a department store. As you descend, the sun, like a lamp on the second floor on which you started, seems to slowly get higher above you. Your escalator trip eventually takes you far enough that you can no longer see the lamp; the sun has "gone down" behind you. When we do this, it becomes clear that *we* are moving relative to the sun, not the sun to us. With enough practice of this sort, our brains will automatically perceive the earth relative to the sun as we know it to be, not as our commonsense perceptions offer us.

Birding is a training in that kind of vision. It is a way of tuning the eyes and ears and mind to a truth in the world that would otherwise go unrecognized. If I told a nonbirder that there were likely ten or more species of birds around them at any given point—and that if they listed all the birds with which they shared space in a given day it would likely be more than fifty species—they would be incredulous. Vision means moving from the raw *seeing* of the world and toward a wider *perception* of its reality.

"Blue Whale!" the call went out, and everyone turned to see where Debi was pointing. An individual of the largest species of animal on earth moved through the water with tremendous power and grace. It was like a moving island. Dolphins with white stripes along their side raced along the side of the boat, clearly enjoying this vessel against which to test their speed. And all around birds swirled, soared, and dove. Life was here in abundance, and it was making itself visible.

The guy with the eBird hat sidled up to me as the boat turned back to get a better look at the whale. "I didn't come here for whales," he said in a low grumble. I was sympathetic, in a way. In a place of such abundance, one can't see everything, and many of the bird species we hoped to see were far more subtle than a whale. But in searching for wild things, it is never an either-or. Many of the most awe-inspiring things I've seen have been on the way to something else. I've seen mountain lions and eight-foot alligators and had close encounters with several bears while searching for birds. Birds were the path, but side trails for a vista are usually worth taking.

"Long-tailed Jaeger, 6 o'clock!" one of the spotters called over the noise of the engine. Like synchronized dancers, a dozen pairs of binoculars swung toward the bird as it moved past the boat. Its sharp beak and powerful build are the sure sign of a predator. One of the spotters offered his own kind of "Pirates of the Caribbean" guide to jaeger identification, matching each of the three most common North American jaeger species to a character in the movie. "The Long-tailed Jaeger is the Jack Sparrow," the spotter said, "because they are dainty, almost floppy in their flight like the character played by Johnny Depp." I could see the resemblance as the bird flew past, almost tern-like in its flight. "Parasitic Jaegers are like Will Turner, slim but well built, while Pomarine Jaegers are like Barbarossa—thicker and heavy set." It had been years since I'd seen the movies, but the basic comparison made sense, especially since jaegers are often referred to as "pirates of the skies."

Similes like these go a long way in learning bird identification, and there are scores of such images across the birding world. Such techniques help clue observers into an aspect of the bird that they could otherwise easily miss. It is not difficult to distinguish jaegers from gulls or terns or shearwaters, but separating the three from one another is considered an advanced identification challenge.

There are two general approaches to such challenges, akin to martial arts—a hard style and a soft style. The hard style is what Pete

Dunne calls the "tertial school," referring to a set of feathers at the very base of the wing that are clear with only a very good look. Birders of this style need to see every field mark, every small detail of the plumage, if they are to count a species on a list. I remember being with a birder of this school looking at a skulking sparrow in a shrub in Big Bend National Park. It was a Black-chinned Sparrow, a bird found in the United States only in a small sliver near the border with Mexico. The bird resembles a Dark-eyed Junco with a black goatee. It's not a terribly hard bird to identify, but this birder would not put it on his life list until he saw every detail. I was a teenager on this trip, and my patience for such exactitude was short. Yet as I've grown older, I've come to appreciate its virtues.

I'm a regional reviewer for eBird, one of a group of volunteers selected to evaluate unusual bird records submitted to Cornell Lab of Ornithology's eBird program. From out-of-season birds to out-of-range birds, eBird reviewers help ensure that the data collected through eBird is reliable and useful for science. In my work as an eBird reviewer, I have become a fan of birders who include the details of their sightings. The best birders give full descriptions, noting how they eliminated similar species, the methods by which they counted the birds (1x1, counted by 10s, etc.), and details about the plumage, structure, and behavior of the bird in question.

Still, at least in the field, I lean toward the other style. Giss, or jizz (yeah, I know), is what birders refer to as an identification made by general impression, size, and shape. Australian birder Sean Dooley describes giss as "the indefinable quality of a particular species, the 'vibe' it gives off." This is the soft style of birding. It relies on experience and intuition.

The first use of the term in print was in 1921, when the British ornithologist Thomas Coward used it in his column for the *Manchester Times*. "If we are walking on the road and see, far ahead, someone whom we recognise although we can neither distinguish features nor particular clothes, we may be certain that we are not mistaken," he wrote. "There is something in the carriage, the walk, the general appearance which is familiar; it is, in fact, the individual's jizz."

Just as we can recognize a good friend from far away, a familiarity with birds renders the same easy naming. This giss or jizz identification can also be taught by pointing out the unique ways certain birds move through the air or hold their bodies. There are ways to describe the impression each species gives, and many of the most groundbreaking advances in bird ID are along those lines. It may not lead to a definitive ID, but it can often send one in the right direction.

Why Coward called it "jizz" no one knows, but there's a chance that it's a corruption of the German *gestalt*, which refers to a shape or form. The discipline of gestalt psychology explores the ways that we can perceive whole patterns, even sometimes completing missing information in order to fit it into the whole. Birding often involves gestalt perceptions—a quick flash of a wing, a bird quickly flying across a road—with our brains taking these bits of information and filling in the missing pieces. This too is part of gaining vision. When we pick up broad mental maps and then see the world through them, our ability to perceive the world is deepened.

The boat had turned toward shore, our allotted time nearing its end, but we kept watching the waves for birds. "Alcid, coming up off the bow," one of the spotters called. Puffins and auklets, razorbills and murres are among the birds in the family alcidae, or alcids, for short. One of the features of jizz birding is the ability to narrow the field of species. It helps to know the general category of bird, and with a bit of experience, you can recognize a bird family or genus, allowing for a more focused probe for the distinct markings of a species. This was my first time to see any alcids in the wild, since most of my birding had been inland, but already I could call them from a distance due to their distinctive shape.

Most of the alcids we encountered were sitting on the water. There were Rhinoceros Auklets, with their aptly named horned bills, and the abundant Common Muirs, with their slender bodies and penguin-like black and white. As we approached this bird, however, it became clear it was something different. "Tufted Puffin!" Shearwater exclaimed as we came close enough to see its markings. *Birds of the World* describes the tufted puffin as the "one member of the auk family whose appearance—like that of a biker in leather regalia—says, 'Don't mess with me!'" I could see it, the bird with its leather-jacket black, its crown decorated liked an edgy haircut. It was immeasurably better than some cold description of "black bird with white mask, orange bill, and feather tufts behind." With the metaphor, the sight of this puffin is transformed into a vision, even in the rearview of memory.

I was glad, looking at the spectacle of this puffin, that I had opted for 10x binoculars. Thanks to a small payout of life insurance after the death of Emily's father earlier in the year, we'd both splurged on equipment upgrades for our trip to California—a top-shelf sleeping bag and new backpack for Emily, new binoculars for me. Zeiss was the brand I quickly settled on, but then came the question of power, what birders call magnification. Magnifications of 8x and 10x are the two major options. For wide angles in close quarters, such as forest birding, 8x is the best, but 10x is best for long distances and open landscapes, like hawk-watching or pelagic birding. Most people go for the do-it-all magnification of 8x. But since my hands are steady, and through years of practice I'm good at getting my binoculars on a bird, I decided I'd go for maximum power. I've been satisfied with that choice, and never more so than on the boat in Monterey Bay. We could have used a spotting scope to get a better look at many of the birds, but the higher the magnification, the more unstable the image becomes. That doesn't work well on a boat in the ocean, where the waves cause constant rocking. So 10x binoculars are about as good as it gets, and seeing a Tufted Puffin in all his biker-style detail was worth it.

Vision begins unaided by learning to interpret the data of mere sight; how to pick out the movement of a warbler, for instance, rather than the rustle of leaves in a breeze. But ever since Galileo and his telescope and van Leeuwenhoek and his microscope, the worlds hidden by distance or size have become seeable and thus new fodder for the work of vision. With the help of lenses and prisms, we can bend light to make the small larger. Binoculars began as two simple telescopes linked together, but it wasn't until the mid-nineteenth century that the Italian inventor Ignazio Porro developed a prism system that significantly improved the resolution of binoculars. His designs were improved and put into commercial production in 1894 by Carl Zeiss.

Eventually Zeiss patented a new design in 1904 using what are called "roof prisms." This design is still the basis of most straight-barreled binoculars, while those with angular designs (what we often think of as the classic binocular look) use the original "Porro prism" design. When I hold the descendant of those original Zeiss binoculars, I can see that a tiny bird, moving among the leaves of a tall oak, is a Yellow-throated Vireo. Thanks to optics, I can also scan a horizon and see a tiny speck that becomes an albatross, the famous ocean bird of poetic fame, flying freely behind the boat.

We saw two species of albatross that day. These giants of the sea are among the most pelagic of all birds, meaning that they go to land only rarely to nest. Debi told us that the Black-footed Albatross that we were seeing could have a nest in Hawaii. It had flown here, all the way to California, to forage for food that it would then bring back to its young. "As the crow flies" is a helpful metaphor for a distance as measured by the flight of a bird, but "as the albatross flies" offers a whole new spatial reality.

"Storm petrel!" a guide called. I followed his arm, pointing to a spot 45 degrees off the front of the boat. Looking at bird books, I'd always imagined these birds to be larger, but it was barely the size of a robin. It seemed impossible that such a small bird, dwarfed by the expanse of the sea, could be a pelagic specialist—and yet it was.

The guide who'd called the petrel was young, his hair a shaggy blond, with a long-lensed camera slung at his side and binoculars around his neck. He was leading a small group on a birding tour of California. They had joined Shearwater's trip as part of their itinerary, since Monterey Bay was a must-see California hotspot. The guide was good, clearly an experienced pelagic birder, and he joined Debi and her spotters in calling out species as we went, all the while focusing on making sure his customers got on the birds. Watching as he worked to show birds to those he was guiding, I admired his skill at pointing.

Showing a bird to someone else, to get their vision to match ours, is difficult. You can try the clock method or naming some fixed point nearby. But often the best way to show someone a bird is to call out the name of the bird, come alongside them, and point over their shoulder, so that they can follow your extended arm to the exact place you are indicating.

When God was a bird, God came as a dove. The point was to show humans something—an otherwise invisible energy and reality—at the heart of the world.

If you forget or have never heard that story, it goes like this. John the Baptist (or literally, John the Dipper) was a wilderness prophet. He lived off wild foods directly from creation. His message to the people living around the region of Judea was to change their hearts and lives, and he told them that one day a person would come who would usher in a completely new way of life. Then one day John's cousin, Jesus, who was beginning to live into the role of a Jewish rabbi, or teacher, came to John to be baptized in the Jordan River, the primary vein of Israel's watershed. Jesus, John told the crowd, was the one he'd been talking about. When John baptized Jesus, something strange happened. As the Gospel of Mark puts it: "And just as he was coming up out of the water, he saw the heavens torn apart and the Spirit descending like a dove on him. And a voice came from heaven, 'You are my Son, the Beloved; with you I am well pleased'" (Mark 1:10–11).

For Christians, the Holy Spirit (or more literally, the Holy Breath) is God—a member of the Trinity. So when this Spirit of God descended as a dove, God took the form of a bird. This bird came to show the crowd by the Jordan River that Jesus, the carpenter from Nazareth, was something more than a mere rabbi, that he contained a fullness not easily perceived by eyes trained in a different kind of looking.

Later, when Jesus was talking to his disciples about the person of God who would come and be with them after Jesus left, he named this Holy Breath that had taken the form of a dove the "Parakaleo." This is the word for the Holy Spirit that John's Gospel uses. It is a linking of the Greek prefix *para*, meaning "alongside," and *kaleo*, which means "call out."

The third person of God is the one who comes beside us and helps us see what we otherwise couldn't. The Spirit is one who points and reveals and says, "Look there!"

To have vision, we need someone to come alongside us and call out. Without such people, we would miss a greater seeing, a deeper vision. Just as it would be easy for a birder to look at the leaves of a damp forest floor and miss the bulbous eyes of a woodcock without the help of another birder, so it is easy for us to miss the truth of the world—its light and hope—amid the visual noise around us. Vision requires community. That, too, is a spiritual truth. We don't find the truth all by ourselves but in conversation and looking alongside others. I'm sure I could have had a fine day of birding in Monterey Bay if I'd gone by myself on a whale tour and found what birds I could. But there is no way I would have seen as much.

And that's true in my home birding haunts as well, where I'm familiar with the landscape. Just as I was completing this chapter, a rare bird was found at a local lake. I went with a group of birders from around Arkansas to see it, and by the end of an hour, together we'd found not one rare bird but four. It was all of us, helping one another see, that filled out our vision of the wild, swirling world of birds around us.

By a couple of hours into the Monterey Bay trip, I was beginning to see for myself, spotting birds and calling them out. The seascape was becoming more legible, as I slowly learned to decipher its language. The writer David Abram argues for a recovery of an animate understanding of the world. There is an aliveness all around us that is speaking; we simply can't hear it. I listened to an interview with Abram in which he tried to show that this idea—that inanimate things have a voice—is not so wild or strange. To demonstrate, he pointed to our ability to read and write. "Writing is magic," said Abram. The alphabet, he adds, "is a very potent form of magic, a very concentrated form of animism." He goes on to explain:

> *For our Indigenous ancestors, one could be wandering through the terrain and have one's attention snagged by a boulder with patches of crinkly black and red lichen spreading on their surface, and you would focus your eyes on a patch of lichen and abruptly hear the rock speaking to you. Well, that's not so different from us waking up in the morning, walking to the kitchen, opening up the paper, and focusing our eyes on a few bits of ink on the page, and suddenly we hear voices and we see visions of events happening in the White House or in Iraq. We focus our eyes on these ostensibly inanimate bits of ink on the page and we hear voices, conversations unfolding between people on the far side of the world.*

We learn to read pages, and we can learn to read the wild world, once again, as well. We just have to have the vision to see it as a text, a meaningful gathering of matter, rather than a voiceless, spiritless void.

The question, as Jesus so often asked his followers, is whether we have eyes to see and ears to hear. This wasn't a question of equipment; it was a question of vision and listening. Could they learn to witness the world around with true vision, a sensitivity to the world that is both skill and grace? Can we? Birding has taught me to experience a hint of this more-than-seeing, this ability to witness a deeper reality of the world. I have only experienced hints of this, and I know there is a good deal that I am missing.

After hours on the ocean, just as my eyes were becoming adjusted to the expanse, the boat began its journey back. We continued counting the birds, adding new species as we went—an Arctic Tern, a tiny bird on its way from one pole of the earth to the other; a Merlin, a small falcon flying for whatever reason over the expanse of the Pacific; a hummingbird, even, that at one point flew past. It was a wonder-filled day, and I left with a wider view, not only of birds and all the places they make their life but of my place in the vast expanse of creation.

Sometimes to really see is to recognize that there is so much that I cannot see. I must remain open, letting my eyes adjust, and listening for the voice that comes alongside and says: look there!

10

OCTOBER

Patience

BELOW ME, A wren is working a tangle of wild grapes and beautyberries, its trills echoing against the sandstone. The day is warm for mid-October, the sun bright in a cloudless sky. The color of the sky is a shade my friend Cameron and I labeled "Broad-wing Blue" while we were hawk-watching on afternoons after high school. It is a shade of deep indigo into which high-flying hawks, like Broad-wings, can easily disappear.

A good day for seeing hawks is when towering cumulonimbus arrive with a cold front, the hawks riding the front south, visible against the whites and grays. This fall, there have been few of those clouds and little rain. This has been a dry, sunny, and warm season—different, changed from those I can remember thirty years ago.

By now, most of the Broad-wings have gone. Their swirling kettles, formed around the thermal columns of warm air rising from the earth, carried them far south to a winter in the northern Amazon of Brazil, or the dense forests of Colombia. The last time I saw a large movement of hawks in kettles, I was camping on St. Francis Day in early October along the Big Piney River in the Ozark Mountains. A cold front came through and with it, swirling groups of Broad-wings. Birders call these groups "kettles" because when the numbers of hawks are large enough (and they can number in the hundreds), they resemble a cooking pot in the sky. They're like a witch's cauldron of feathers and flesh. It takes some imagination, sure. But imagination isn't hard to come by when you're lying on your back for hours looking up. The mind searches for meaning, patterns, and shapes, and the sky is often gracious to provide.

Some raptors, like Sharp-shinned Hawks, flap their wings often, powering their flight through bursts of energy. But Broad-wings have been known to ride the elevators of thermals, gliding from one to the next to the next for hundreds of miles without moving their wings. They are a wonder. But many days, when I watch the sky in the fall, there is no movement. Still, I wait for those moments when suddenly—abundance!

Today, so far, I am still waiting for the arrival. All I see are a couple of Turkey Vultures, cruising the ridgeline. Common, strange, ugly by most standards, these vultures have their own kind of charm. They are marvelous flyers, and I've heard many nonbirders mistake their majestic paths for those of an eagle. I usually let them believe what they like. Eagles, after all, are just as ready to chow down on roadkill. One of the easiest places to find a Bald Eagle is outside of a chicken farm where the dead broilers are tossed in a pile, ready to be picked up by our national bird.

Waiting and watching go together. And hawk-watching, like a form of silent prayer, embodies them more than most other forms of birding. To see warblers in the tops of oak trees with their leaves just budding, or sparrows in a winter field, the standing grass stalks a rusty brown, requires moving: walking around in the landscape, listening carefully to what the sounds of the birds reveal. Shorebirding and duck watching often involve driving, stopping at various points on a lake to scope or scan a muddy field. In all of these the mind is busy, the body active. But hawk-watching is mostly a stillness. Like a monk on a mountain, you have to sit before a big sky and wait for what might come.

Hawks sometimes call as they fly, but usually hawk-watching is just that—a purely visual activity. My method, one learned on long afternoons in my teens, is to sit some place where I can see the full expanse of the northern horizon. First I look with my eyes, scanning like I read, left to right, moving up the sky from the horizon to as far as I feel like tilting my head. Then I do the same with my binoculars, focused in on some far point in the distance. I follow the white edge of the horizon, moving left to right, up and then right to left—the blue deepening in its shades as I go up.

I wait and repeat, keeping my eyes fixed on the horizon. It is surprising how a hawk can suddenly appear, even after you've just looked across an unobscured expanse of sky. One day, sitting on this same ridge a few weeks before, I suddenly saw a pair of American Kestrels above me, chattering to one another as they cleared the cliffs. I'd been keeping watch carefully, but they came seemingly from nowhere. Just as quickly they disappeared.

These small falcons are year-round residents in Arkansas, but many migrate from the north to winter here or farther south in Texas. As with all falcons, they are dynamic birds, fast flyers that carry in their bodies a kind of Top-Gun confidence. Kestrels are the daintiest of the North American falcons. Yet seeing them in migration, you know their power.

I've never been to one of the big North American hawk watches, like those at Hawk Mountain in Pennsylvania or the platform at Cape May, New Jersey. There, in season, the hawks come in streams and floods. During the seasons, these major hawk watches host professional birders with clickers on their fingers, tallying raptors in the thousands.

At one time, Hawk Mountain in Pennsylvania had been a place where hawks were killed by the scores. Already noting the loss of songbirds, some nineteenth-century ornithologists mistakenly believed that culling the hawk population was part of the solution to helping songbirds thrive. Since many hawks hunt smaller birds, they concluded that it was an overabundance of hawks instead of habitat loss that was to blame. This faulty knowledge became the standard practice of conservation, though it ended up conserving nothing. To know that history is a warning against hubris, a call to be humble in our science, and in our presumption that we know what is good for the birds. As with most things, the reality is more complicated than we think. Like our watching, our understanding and actions must remain tenuous. This, too, is a lesson in waiting.

I've seen significant movements of hawks in Arkansas, but always there has been a flow of ups and downs. Hawk-watching for me has involved mostly waiting for long stretches. But sometimes, without warning, the sky is filled with migrating hawks that pass in swirling wonder. Then the sky, once again, is suddenly empty. This waiting, this watching, is forged in hope.

In the Christian scriptures, there's a beautiful line about waiting from St. Paul's letter to the church in Rome. This church is a community in crisis, suffering from ethnic divisions and the pressures of a vicious empire. To this group of people he writes, "if we hope for what we do not see, we wait for it with patience" (Romans 8:25). That word, *patience*, in the Greek of the New Testament, could also be translated as *persistence*. Whether patience or persistence, those words could easily be the mantra of a hawk watcher. We wait patiently in hope for what we do not now see, persistently watching for hours on end. And if we wait with hope, sometimes, like a miracle, we will see the extraordinary.

Persistence is a necessary element of hope. It is easy, when faced with the challenges of the world, the big problems that can seem so overwhelming, to simply give up. And yet the most hopeful actions on behalf of hawks and raptors came through the persistent efforts of a few people. It required persistence on the part of scientists and rehabilitators to bring back the California Condor from the brink of extinction. From a population that had plummeted to merely twenty-seven individuals in 1987, this creature once again soars above the western sky in many parts of its historic range. And it took the persistence of people like Rachel Carson to ban the chemicals that were pushing raptors like Bald Eagles, Ospreys, and Peregrine Falcons to near extinction. This persistence was not a dogged pursuit for the sake of some personal gain but was instead a patient work of hope in action.

That is what waiting for hope with persistence is all about. And sometimes, the reward comes flying over.

I remember, as a teenager, reading an essay by Pete Dunne, who founded the Cape May hawk watch, in which he recounted a day on the platform at the Cape May Bird Observatory in New Jersey. After years of low numbers of Peregrine Falcons, suddenly, on that fall day, falcons came through in abundance. Hundreds of them poured through the sky that year. All that time, through the thin years, the watchers had been persistent in their counting—counts that helped measure what was happening to the falcons. Now, a few years into the ban on DDT, the falcons were recovering in abundance. Hope was alive.

In that passage of Paul's letter, just a few lines before speaking of hope, he writes that creation "groans in eager longing." The wild world is waiting to live into fullness and flourishing, a fullness that is now put in check by human exploitation. In such a world, it is easy to give up waiting and the hope always hidden within it.

A friend of mine, a birder in his eighties who has been watching birds since he was teenager, once remarked that I find more falcons and eagles than he does. In wondering about it, he said that he thinks it is because he long ago gave up looking for them. For so much of his younger life, he simply knew that they were not to be expected. And yet now I see them, sometimes even in abundance. Just the other day, five Bald Eagles gathered on the shore of the lake below me. What birds could be brought back if only we joined hope and persistence with the work of restoration?

I continue my scan, and just as I move my binoculars to the right, I catch the speck of a raptor against the blue. It is far away, a couple of miles at least. Still, I watch carefully, paying attention to its shape, the way it holds its wings, what color I can catch. The wings are fairly broad and rounded toward their end, its tail clearly extending from its body but not long. This is the general shape of hawks belonging to the *Buteo* genus. Broad-winged, Red-tailed, and Red-shouldered Hawks are its most common members in this area. Getting the genus is an important first step in the process of elimination, which is a big part of identification.

As the hawk banked and I saw it head on, I could see that the wings undulated slightly, dipping from the shoulders, cresting, then dipping and rising again slightly at the tips. Each bird has a different shape, a different way of holding its wings. With enough practice and experience, you can learn to distinguish them. I'd first been educated in the techniques of this kind of identification by the book *Hawks in Flight*, but it is long experience with these birds that had given me the confidence to make a call. Like seeing an old friend at a distance, picking up their distinct gait, it is not all analysis. Somehow, beyond a clear list of reasons, you just know who they are. It becomes that way with birds, after a while, even at a long distance. This is an example of "jizz" or "giss" birding at its best. "Red-tailed Hawk," I said to myself, watching the bird and waiting for it to come closer for a sure confirmation.

In college, I took some classes in photography. This was back in the day of film and darkrooms. I loved learning to develop my own prints, entering that strange space of red light and the sound of dripping water, the vinegar odor of the stop-bath chemicals filling the air. I loved how the prints dried like laundry on a clothesline, attached with wooden clips on lines running around the edges of the room.

The most magical moment of the darkroom was placing the exposed photo paper in the developer trays. The chemicals would react with the silver halides that had been exposed to the reversed light of the negative. Slowly, like a ghost arriving from another realm, the image would appear beneath the liquid. It was the moment of truth: Did the photograph work or not? Was the exposure a good one? In the waiting was a kind of mystery.

Photography has largely gone the way of the digital—instant images, with no wait to wonder how they turned out—but hawk-watching is still an act of waiting for the resolution. Was my call right? It's a matter of wait and see. In this case, the bird came more quickly than I expected, pushed forward by the north wind, its red tail a clear giveaway. I'd been right; the image had resolved.

I continued to watch, pausing to crack open the pistachios I'd grabbed as a quick lunch. At some point, the watching doesn't become about seeing the hawks anymore. It is an invitation to silence, like a prayer that runs out of words and becomes only an open waiting. "Silence," wrote R. S. Thomas in his poem "The Untamed," "Holds with its gloved hand / The wild hawk of the mind."

Below me is an area designated as a state wildlife management area. In a few weeks hunters will climb into the trees and sit, waiting for deer. It's a more common pursuit in these parts than birding, but the two cross over easily. Many of the best birders I know started as hunters.

I've never hunted, but when I talk to friends who go to the "deer woods," many admit that what they love isn't the actual hunt but the waiting. "I just like the peace of sitting out on the deer stand," more than one friend has told me. Sometimes we need permission, in a world of hurry and demands of productivity, to sit and wait and watch. Hunting, fishing, and birding are forms of that permission—an allowance to be quiet and sit.

We might think this is a modern problem, born of capitalism and the industrial economy, but it seems our problem with patient waiting goes back even further. In seventeenth-century England, one of the most popular books was Sir Izaak Walton's *The Compleat Angler, or The Contemplative Man's Recreation*. "Money-getting men," writes Walton, "spend all their time, first in getting, and next, in anxious care to keep it. . . . We Anglers," he says, "pity them perfectly, and stand in no need to borrow their thoughts to think ourselves so happy." Instead, Walton invites us to stand before rivers, which, he says, "are made for wise men to contemplate and for fools to pass by without consideration."

The same could be said for a mountain ridge or a hawk watch platform. Against the rushing world demanding always more, we step away and contemplate the sky. We may even feel a hint of pity for those who can't catch the joy of watching.

Then, without announcement, the wait is over. As I adjust my back against the rocks, a bird rises over the ridge, wings beating in quick pumps and moving to a glide. The shape, its long tail and wings spread at the tips, give it away as a hawk of the *Accipiter* genus. Coopers or Sharp-shinned? This bird is small, its tail squared off at the corners, so it must be a Sharp-shinned Hawk, the less common of the two species in this region. My heart jumps at the sight, as the bird disappears just as quickly down into the trees below. I pull out my phone and log it into eBird.

Silence, then sudden thrill—that is the pattern. Birding is a mashup of monastery and casino: contemplation turning to the ring of the jackpot. And like gambling, birding stimulates a powerful system of reward. Slot machines are engineered to provide intermittent rather than regular rewards. Our brains are wired not for predictable returns but for repeated efforts that sometimes (but not always) bring a big result. It's an addictive process, one casinos build into their games, but I think it has a deeper purpose going back to our hunting and gathering ancestors. If we just kept hunting as long as we were rewarded with game, then we'd quit easily when nothing showed up. It is the random, occasional reward that keeps us coming. It is this kind of primal patience that helps us stay through the waiting.

But this patience, this deep persistence, is also at the heart of all mystical pursuits. We keep showing up in the world with quiet prayers and meditations. So often, for months and even years at a time, this showing up results in nothing. We're just waiting. And then, epiphany! We see a light we wouldn't have encountered if we hadn't been watching, waiting, getting our eyes ready to see.

It could be said that the root of all our problems comes from the inability to wait. That, at least, is how Blaise Pascal put it. The seventeenth-century gambler and mathematician became a Christian and took up residence in a monastery. There he worked on a book on the nature of life and faith. He jotted down little notes for the book on scraps of paper and put them in a drawer. Pascal died before he could put the book together, but the collected scraps, called his *Pensées* or "Thoughts," contain a treasury of insight. Among the most famous of those scraps is this: "I have often said that the sole cause of man's unhappiness is that he does not know how to stay quietly in his room."

It's a thought worth pondering quietly, alone in a room, or at least considering on a mountain ridge where no humans are about. What Pascal is getting at is that there is something deep within us that cannot stand waiting. We often prefer chaos and disaster to waiting one more minute. To escape the wait, we also tend to turn toward distractions, settling for the junk food of body and mind rather than staying hungry for what will truly satisfy us.

Such an inability to wait is at the heart of the Jewish story of the Exodus. After the people of Israel are liberated from the pharaoh of Egypt who made them work relentlessly, making bricks for palaces and pyramids, the people find themselves in the stark emptiness of the wilderness. Looking for instruction, Moses goes up Mount Sinai to hear what they are to do next. He's gone a long while, and in the waiting, the people decide to make their own god, one they can control—a golden calf. It doesn't end well, but it was all because they couldn't persist with hope. Moses hadn't come, and they thought it time to make a god they could control.

Another French philosopher, several centuries later, commented on this link between waiting and idolatry. Jacques Derrida, in his lectures on hospitality, wrote: "Those who make idols are not those who know how to wait; they themselves need to produce what they wait for, to produce gods. In other words, the break with idolatry consists not only in not making images; it also consists in knowing how to wait." I can imagine Derrida in the lecture hall of a Parisian university, his shock of white hair combed back, his expressive eyebrows furrowed as he takes a toke from his tobacco pipe and says: "Not knowing how to wait is idolatry, it is to produce from oneself what one wants to allow to come."

Not knowing how to wait is idolatry, and it is also violence. Without waiting, we move quickly, acting with speed. "Speed," as the theologian Stanley Hauerwas has put it, "is just another name for violence." Patience, then, is training in nonviolence, non-coercion. It knows that while justice and goodness and beauty are urgent needs in the world, neither can they be forced or manufactured without undermining their very existence. To learn patience is to learn that the world is not ours to bend to our whims, that others are not objects to control for our purposes. Like the Holy Spirit, known at times to come as a bird, the wind blows where it will. And in the waiting, when all seems over, the magic comes.

I think this is part of the reason I haven't been much of what birders call a "chaser" as an adult. No worries if driving at the drop of a hat to respond to a rare bird alert is your thing. I get the thrill, and clearly sometimes I follow it. But for me, unless it is truly, wildly rare, I don't usually bother going to look for a bird someone else has found. I prefer finding rare birds no one has yet reported. There may be some ego in this—it is nice to see my name first on the eBird alerts to which serious birders subscribe that let them know when an unusual bird has been found in their state or county. But more deeply, I enjoy the patient sorting through of a raft of ducks to find a Black Scoter bobbing in their midst, or the sense that a sandbar in a riverside park where Ring-billed Gulls gather in the hundreds will one day also include a Lesser Black-backed Gull. Most days, these visits return nothing. Most days I go and look and wait and simply enjoy the common beauty of the birds I know but whose lives are so separate and different from my own.

Below me, as I sit on the ridge, I can hear the voices of a group of hikers. The ridge I'm on is not part of any trail. Still, it is on the summit, and I hope that I won't be found. To the east of me there is another mountain ridge. It's a popular state park where hundreds of people hike each weekend.

I was there a few weeks ago, on a hike with my wife. That day we sat, quietly, watching toward the north. Broad-wings were on the move, a handful circling low over the peak, mixed with a group of Black Vultures rising on the same thermal.

A group of young people came up. They were blasting music from their phones, taking selfies as soon as they hit the summit. Not far away, a young woman pulled a drone from her backpack and sent it flying as she lifted her arms out in a "top of the mountain" pose, ready to snap the perfect Instagram shot. My wife and I sat amid the clatter and noise waiting for the return to silence. It didn't take long. They got their selfies, no need to linger with the vistas.

Patience is a path toward presence. Presence, it seems, is in short supply these days. I feel it in myself: a restlessness to look elsewhere, to pick up my phone, to switch tabs on my computer, to see if another email has come in since I checked five minutes ago. One way I work against this tendency is to find time to sit on ridges like this. Patience is often perfected in the crucible of solitude. I make a point, at least once a month, to spend half a day in solitude. Hawk-watching is a good way to live into this commitment, although sometimes it is simply a long hike or run. No headphones, limited use of my phone, just a solitary presence to the wild world around me.

In their book, *Lead Yourself First*, Raymond Kethledge and Michael Erwin define solitude as a time when the mind is "isolated from the input of other minds." It's a helpful framing that I might revise to freedom from the input of *human* minds. That means that when I'm in solitude, I have no human companion, I'm not reading, I'm not listening to a podcast or music. But that doesn't mean that I am alone. Every place is full of voices if we listen—from gurgling creeks to raucous Blue Jays to the delicate flutter of a migrating monarch.

Listening and watching: these acts also help me to cut off the constant chatter of my own mind, the voices that are always running their mouths with despairing stories and anxious wonderings. By giving my attention to the rustle of leaves, the flash of movement, the high-pitched song of Golden-crowned Kinglets moving through the tops of the pine trees below the ridge—I am drawn out of myself and into a wholeness in which I get, for a moment, to be a member.

I know of no major religious tradition, no spiritual teaching worth following, that does not place solitude among its key practices. We human beings are social creatures, yes: communal, relational, and connected. That is a good and beautiful thing, mostly. But because of the social nature of our lives, we are often drawn into the anxieties of others, and we can lose ourselves in the crowd. The philosopher Martin Heidegger said that human beings have a temptation to become a "they-self," in which our identity gets completely bound up with some anonymous mass in which we find our meaning. Given that Heidegger became a member of the Nazi party during the rise of the Third Reich, one must wonder if he knew this truth from his own experience.

Dietrich Bonhoeffer, a Christian theologian who lived at the same time as Heidegger and heroically resisted the Nazis, wrote in his book *Life Together*: "Let him who cannot be alone beware of community. . . . Let him who is not in community beware of being alone. . . . Each by itself has profound perils and pitfalls. One who wants fellowship without solitude plunges into the void of words and feelings, and the one who seeks solitude without fellowship perishes in the abyss of vanity, self-infatuation and despair."

To birdwatch in community is a beautiful thing. And to go birding alone is an important balance. Sometimes even the self needs rest from itself. By turning my attention outward, to the vast blue horizon, I get that rest.

I first discovered the joy of solitude when I was in high school. My family lived, at the time, at a conference center where my father was the director. We were on a mountaintop, a flat mesa with hundreds of acres of open grassland pastures and hardwood forests. Every day after I got home from school, I would grab my binoculars and go birding. I didn't do it according to some plan or think of it in terms of a healthy decompression from the day at school. I just went because that's what I longed to do.

In that aloneness I was brought into a greater community of life, one whose patterns shifted with the season, a migrating collection of creatures who shared this place with me for a season or around the year. I learned that in the winter the turkeys would gather into bands, the females and males separated, sometimes running through the fields like the feathered dinosaurs they are. I knew that in the open pine grove, where grasses grew in the dappled light, that I could sometimes find an elusive Bachman's Sparrow in the spring. Then there were the resident birds, the meadowlarks with their bright yellow breasts marked with a black v, who, for all the color of their undersides, could blend in with the grass as they crouched against it with their brown splattered backs. And in the fall, I'd sit on the highest point in the pasture and face north, watching for the hawks that would come overhead, birds that were often joined by migrating monarchs—their orange wings clear against the blue and white of the sky.

While birding in solitude, I have no steady object for my mind to work through. My attention is directed around me, and the problems within are put aside. In a strange and paradoxical way, it is here, lost from my own self, that I can be found. There is a book by the French Christian mystic Pierre de Causade titled *The Sacrament of the Present Moment*, or, in other translations, *Abandonment to Divine Providence*. In it de Causade expresses the truth at the heart of all spiritual seeking:

"That which I might endeavour to find in other ways seeks me incessantly and gives itself to me through all creatures."

That which I seek is seeking me and speaking through all those I encounter. The birds are offering one version of that voice, but I must get quiet enough to hear it.

I look down at the lake beneath me. Bald Eagles live there year around now, nesting in various places at the water's edge, but in this season the resident birds are being joined by migrants from the north. As common as they have become, I never tire seeing them in flight. They dwarf all the other raptors in the region, and for all their foibles (stealing food from smaller birds, eating carrion), they are still majestic.

I spot a pair of eagles below me, soaring over the water. They are likely a breeding pair. As with most raptors, the female is the larger of the two, the male smaller. In terms of plumage, they are identical—white heads and white tails, a chocolate brown body. I can even see the bright yellow of their bills.

When I was in seminary I lived not far from the Potomac River, near Washington, DC. I once saw a Bald Eagle soaring over the river, with the Washington Monument in the background. It seemed a cinematic cliché, or a set piece for a political campaign ad. But the eagle was real and free, doing what it has done for centuries—fishing in a river at the heart of their native range. The Washington Monument was the only thing new about the scene.

It was in seminary that I began to rekindle my love of birding. It was also a time when I began to deepen my spiritual practices, informed in new and deeper ways by what I was studying. One of those practices was fasting—a deliberate refraining from food for a set period of time. Fasting has had a resurgence of late, not as a religious practice but for the sake of health. Taking a break from food can offer various benefits, including initiating processes in which the body rids itself of damaged cells. But trend or not, fasting has long been a part of cultures throughout the world, and like solitude, it is a feature of most major religions.

On many of the days I hike this ridge for the sake of solitude, I do so while fasting. It is an added layer to my training in patience. To fast is to say to myself that I can wait for something I want. We are all wanting things, and that is not bad. Desire is not necessarily a problem within the Christian tradition; in fact, it is something we seek to cultivate in the right direction. But as with all good things, desire can come to dominate us, and the wrong desires can push us astray.

In the distance, just past the lake, I can see plumes of smoke rising. They are from burning brush piles on lots cleared for houses. A development is going in, sprawling mansions with manicured lawns and good views of the lake below. For years the water company has fought hard to keep such housing away. Our water is good, as unpolluted as one could hope, but the lake is beautiful and people want to live near such beauty. So while the near shore is still protected, mansions are going up on the hillsides. They are a symptom of the desire for more, the good desire for housing and beauty that has ballooned beyond the boundaries of common life and ecological health.

To fast is to learn, in a small way and with an everyday want, to be satisfied with what we have. There are few people who will run into physical harm from not eating for a day or even three days (although if you struggle with disordered eating, even if it wouldn't be physically harmful, approach fasting with caution). Fasting is not pleasant. Still, the small difficulty helps form us for the harder times when we will have to forgo what we want for the sake of the world.

Fasting is not an essential aid to birding. Still, many birders I know skip meals simply because they get so focused on and enthralled with their pursuit. But fasting is an expression of patience, a discipline that can help form us for other times when patience is needed, like waiting for a hawk to appear. More importantly, fasting is an act of patience that helps train all those who love the wild world to care for it more fully. By learning this practice (and "practice is just another name for patience," writes Stanley Hauerwas), we are learning to give up a little of what we want for the sake of making room for the rest of creation.

This is a theme we've been talking about, from hospitality to abundance, but it is one we'll turn toward in a deeper way in the next chapter. For now, on those hungry days I sit watching hawks, I hope that I'm learning how to wait for a better world. That, too, is an act of hope.

The consequences of not waiting for a better world are dire. Without waiting, we either accept the half measures and diminished hopes offered to us by a society that does not want to change, or we join in acts of violence that seek to force change. The way of patience is something different from all of that. It is a strange and subversive action that has unsettled empires and could do so again.

"Strange patience" is the phrase that the early Christian Justin Martyr used to explain the surprising success of Christianity in a Roman world that was anything but patient. Despite persecutions, including executions that ended the lives of people like Justin Martyr, Christianity came to grow and thrive in its first centuries.

It wasn't because of some grand marketing plan or celebrity adherents. Instead, Christianity offered a radical alternative to the world around it. Their pagan neighbors noted that Christians had forbearance in their business dealings (like being patient with renters who are past due) and were unusually patient with those who owed them money; in fact, they would often forgive debts entirely. Their neighbors found this strange but also intriguing. Strange patience often turned curiosity toward conversion.

What if patience once again became the means of creating an alternative to the ways of empire, with all its focus on dominance and control, its seeking of wealth and power? What if learning to be patient was also a lesson in joining with a deeper rhythm at the heart of the world, what the agrarian writer Gene Logsdon called "living at nature's pace"? I'd like to think patience holds such promise. And I know that one part of my learning it is in coming each fall to sit on a ridge for hours on end and watch the horizon.

Eventually the day's heat climbed, and responsibilities at home and work beckoned. I stood up, stretched my stone-contorted back, and slung my backpack over my shoulders for the descent. I gave one more look across the sky. A couple of Black Vultures, with their silver-tipped wings and short tails, soared above. No other hawks were around; the season, it seemed, had mostly passed. Next year, I thought to myself, I'll come and sit again.

11

NOVEMBER

Kenosis

THE SLIGHT SMELL of methane rises from the bank, the sign of anaerobic bacteria beneath the mud, turning the rot of leaves into soil. Growing from that mud, all along the waterline, are horsetails. A food for Jurassic dinosaurs, horsetails are an ancient plant. Rub a penny against them, and it will turn bright from the silica. Cattails line the shore, too, their roots submerged in the water. Both horsetails and cattails are edible, a feature I note whenever I'm by the water. I've never tried either. But if the systems that keep the groceries flowing to the stores ever crash, I want to know where to come for food.

Across the water is a sandbar tucked within an inlet. To its left a milk crate's cubed corner peeks above the waterline, and beyond that emerges some bent metal wreckage, perhaps the legs of a backyard grill. When the floods come, this place is the filter of the river—cattails and sand bars catching the waste. Because it is protected from the rest of the river's flow, the water here is calm, even when the main channels are chaotic. I've never waded into the water here, but I have watched fishermen do so, and so it seems that it is mostly shallow beneath.

Given the number of birds that settle here, the protected waters must also be a place of life—fish and crustaceans moving through the water. Ducks and cormorants, gulls and terns and pelicans, along with migrating shorebirds in due season—this is a place where the resident wildlife seem to have it easy.

There's an old bit of dock, down a little trail through the horsetails—a simple wooden platform on large pads of Styrofoam. I suppose some fisherman constructed it, because it doesn't seem sophisticated enough to have been put here by the parks department. At one time this area was a penal farm for the county—a place of forced labor on a swampy edge of the city. For years it lay fallow. As a teenager I'd come here with other birders (with or without official permission, I'm not sure). It was a place to find Marsh Wrens and Virginia Rails in the spring. The fields hosted LeConte's Sparrows with bright orange faces, but seeing them required braving a walk through a field full of sandburs that collect on socks and shoelaces with their sharp, hooked barbs.

Now the area has been turned into a thriving park, popular with cyclists and families on any sunny weekend. Still, thankfully, there are hidden side trails that are not well traveled, guarded by enough snakes in the summer and spiders in the fall to make them unappealing for many. I follow the trail to the wooden platform and set up my tripod, balancing its feet on the deck to begin my search across the water.

On the sandbar there are twenty large masses of white and black, a bit of yellow poking through here and there. These birds dwarf the Great Egrets nearby, even with their long bills tucked beneath their feathers. They are American White Pelicans, a largely inland species that nests along the Great Lakes and inland rivers in the East, with a sizable population on the Great Salt Lake in the West. I'm not certain where the birds that come to Arkansas each winter nest, but late fall always comes with their arrival—their massive bodies gliding in v shapes above. According to the most widely held theory of their origins, birds are the evolutionary progeny of dinosaurs. To look at a pelican is to see the evidence of that older form. They look like a creature from a different eon.

Many people tell me of their encounters with pelicans on the river. "Shouldn't they be on the ocean?" they ask, eyes wide. Like many species of gulls that are far from limited to the "sea" so often attached to their name, American White Pelicans are a largely inland species.

They are water birds, ravenous fish eaters, and happy to follow the food wherever it is. Brown Pelicans are coastal specialists, but their larger white-and-black cousins love a river sandbar as much as a beach.

In Europe and the river deltas of the Fertile Crescent, pelicans are known as marshland birds. While smaller species are easy to ignore, pelicans make their presence known. They are what might be called "charismatic megafauna," like elephants and lions. It is hard not to miss them and their odd-seeming proportions, dramatic wingspans, and sometimes mystifying behavior. These have been recorded throughout history, from the Hebrew Scriptures to the myths of medieval bestiaries. In Hebrew, the very word for pelican reflects its odd nature. They are called *qa'at* in the Bible, a term that could also mean owl. Both birds were considered unclean because of their habit of vomiting up food to feed their young (a trait that is actually shared by most birds except for those precocial species like chickens and turkeys whose young can feed themselves after hatching).

Nonetheless, the pelican was also a favorite bird of early Christian art, in which it symbolizes God's sacrificial love. I first encountered this enduring symbol when I was in the sanctuary of a Roman Catholic Church in the suburbs of Chicago. It was a massive, neo-Baroque space, full of marble and gold paint, that belonged to a missionary order of priests. On the floor of the sanctuary, just before the altar, was a pelican illustrated in mosaic tile. It was white and black, like the American White Pelicans I see each November, with its long yellow bill turned toward itself. There was one difference, however, from the pelicans I saw gathered on the sandbar. This mosaic pelican's white chest was marked with a patch of red, from which drops of blood poured.

The image represents an ancient belief that was captured in the bestiaries of the ancient world. Bestiaries were books that offered descriptions of animals, mixing zoology with moral and myth (with an emphasis on the last two). It was believed that a mother pelican would revive her dead chicks with her own blood—or as the medieval mystic-scientist Hildegard von Bingen relates it: "When the pelican first sees her chicks hatch from her eggs, she thinks they are not related to her and kills them. When she sees that they do not move, she is sad and lacerates herself, resuscitating them with her blood." It was an imaginative reading of what was likely a common scene in the marshlands of the Mediterranean. Anyone who has ever watched a nest of young birds knows that the birds lie listless, their skin fragile and translucent, seemingly dead. Pelicans, along with most species, excepting chickens, quail, turkeys, and the like, are what are called *altricial*—"requiring nourishment from the parent." When the parent arrives at the nest with food, the chicks suddenly pop up, mouths open, seemingly resurrected.

Reading this scene with imagination, the ancients saw a story of parental self-sacrifice. When Christians inherited this story from the Roman "naturalists," it wasn't a big leap to make a connection with the story of Christ. In his hymn, "*Adoro te devote*," Saint Thomas Aquinas went so far as to say, "Lord Jesus, Good Pelican."

Something stirred the birds on the sandbar, the pelicans rising along with nearby cormorants and Gadwalls. Adult pelicans don't have many predators, due to their size, so perhaps this flight into the air was in solidarity more than fear. When a group of birds gathered on a sandbar or mudflat suddenly lifts from the ground, I've trained my vision to look up. Sometimes it's only a plane or a vulture that has scared them, but often enough I see a falcon or an eagle. In this case, it was a mature Bald Eagle, dark bodied, with its classic white head and tail. Ducks are a favorite eagle food, but this bird plunged toward the river and emerged with a fish instead, bringing momentary calm as it flew to a sycamore on the opposite bank to enjoy its prey.

The action that would cause Hildegard and Thomas Aquinas to compare Christ to a bird was Jesus's sacrificial death for the sake of the world. That God would sacrifice himself is called, in theological terms, *kenosis*. It is a word that that comes from a hymn that Christians were evidently singing a few decades after Jesus's death. We find the verses preserved in Paul's letter to the Philippian church. After a dust-up involving people seeking honor and one-upmanship, Paul was trying to plead with this group of disciples to live in the way Christ did, following his pattern of humility and forgiveness. In a rising call, filled with rhetorical flourish, Paul breaks forth with what would have been a familiar song: "[Christ], though he existed in the form of God, did not regard equality with God as something to be grasped, but emptied himself, taking the form of a slave, assuming human likeness" (Philippians 2:6–7 NRSV). In the Greek of the New Testament, that word *empty* is rooted in the word *kenosis*: to empty oneself, to give oneself over. It captures the whole movement of what Christians understand Christ to have done: give up power, let go of a divine life in heaven, and instead live in the fragile limits of human life, all for the sake of love and healing.

The spring before watching the returning pelicans on that sandbar, I read a story in the *New York Times* by writer Terry Tempest Williams. A Utah native, Williams was writing of the fate of her beloved Great Salt Lake. "From a distance, it is hard to tell whether the three figures walking the salt playa are human, bird or some other animal," she writes. "Through binoculars, I see they are pelicans, juveniles, gaunt and emaciated without water or food. In feathered robes, they walk with the focus of fasting monks toward enlightenment or death. . . . This was not a dream or a nightmare, but the first time I realized Great Salt Lake was in danger of disappearing."

Williams goes on to explain that Gunnison Island in the Great Salt Lake is one of the largest American White Pelican rookeries in the country. Like herons, egrets, and a number of other birds, pelicans nest in large colonies that host as many as twenty thousand nesting birds. The island had been an ideal place for keeping eggs and helpless nestlings safe, protected from land-roving predators like coyotes by a barrier of water on all sides. But with the lake drying up, paths were opened up for predators to visit the island and pick off the easy prey of pelican nestlings. The juvenile pelicans, those emaciated, "fasting monks" Williams saw on the cracked mud of the salt playa, were likely the fleeing refugees of a coyote incursion.

The image of those birds wandering toward death across the dried-out lake is a reminder of the stark realities upon us. As birders know, even abundant species can collapse, a common bird spiraling toward extinction. The Passenger Pigeon was once the most abundant bird in North America, with up to five billion individuals. Passenger Pigeons comprised almost a quarter of the continent's birds. Their migrating flocks would sometimes, famously, black out the sky. And yet the last Passenger Pigeon died alone on September 1, 1914, in a cage at the Cincinnati Zoo. Her species was wiped from the planet by deforestation and reckless hunting.

Abundance has often been an alluring excuse for plunder. To the settler-colonial mind, the Americas seemed an endless land, with forests without border and animals that never ran out. But such abundance relied on a common exchange of life, the cycles of growth and decay, death and birth in balance. It could not stand the pure annihilation of the consumerist mode the colonists brought. And the extractive impulse continues to bring chaos to the systems of life.

Drought and fire, blazing heat and disease, flooding and hail—such events put many species in peril. Combine these climactic events with the continued destruction of habitats through the taming of rivers, the draining of wetlands, and the paving-over of pastures, and extinction becomes a possibility.

We can't take abundance for granted. The canary in the coal mine of our common life on earth may be a dying pelican on a waterless lake.

The inlet of the river now has seven Great Egrets, spread around the shallow waters. White with yellow bills and a striking green around their eyes in breeding season, these birds seem like the elegant cousins of the lopsided pelicans. Though they are not closely related in the current taxonomies, they are often found in similar habitats—both feeding on fish.

It was egrets like these that helped launch the modern bird conservation movement, and they remain the symbol of the National Audubon Society. That society began in 1905, in part to change fashion. Hats were in vogue at the time, the gaudier the better, and the beautiful long plumes of egrets were a favorite adornment. During their breeding season, Great Egrets' normally lush white feathers grow more intricate, with beautiful spirals and curls spilling out in extravagant wonder. But beauty in an extractive world can be a dangerous thing. Rather than simply enjoying the feathers on the birds, hat makers encouraged the mass slaughter of egrets so that those feathers could be owned for the sake of style.

Soon, thankfully, some people began to reject and resist the prevailing fashion. Cousins and socialites Harriet Hemenway and Mina Hall organized tea parties for wealthy women in Gilded-Age Boston to encourage a boycott of feathered hats. Their tea parties eventually became the Massachusetts Audubon Society, a group that banded together with other such groups in New York City and elsewhere to form what is now the National Audubon Society. The egrets were saved.

But the list of those birds that have gone extinct is a long and growing one. And as the perils become more complex, so, too, do the solutions. Stopping the mass slaughter of egrets is one thing. Stopping the inundation of rising seas in a marsh is another. Each species is an exquisite answer to the opportunities of an ecosystem. Some are broad answers, like Northern Cardinals, while others are very specific, like Swainson's Warblers. Northern Cardinals can live in a deep forest or suburban landscape, as long as there is ample seed to be had and insects to feed their young. Swainson's Warblers, however, nest in the very specific habitat of riparian cane breaks. A loss of those cane breaks would mean the loss of the Swainson's Warbler.

Though the warbler is not threatened now, the introduction of pests from shipping containers from China is causing mass die-offs of cane in some places. Increased hurricanes could also destroy habitat and disrupt nesting. No one yet knows. But when a species is specialized, it is more vulnerable to a matrix of threats.

The weaving of this matrix is an outgrowth of the current arrangement of human life on earth, especially the industrialization of everything. Simply put, our demand for endless economic growth and production, driven by the millennia of stored fossil fuel energy that is being burned through in a matter of mere decades, has begun to exhaust the life of the world. And I find little hope in the so-called green economy, particularly since so much of it simply continues in an extractive pattern. It is akin to the balance transfers of a household living off credit. To move from the fossil-fuel economy to the lithium one is simply transferring the balance from one credit card to another. The interest rate may be lower for now, but it too will eventually grow beyond what we can afford. The only real answer is to learn to live below our means and begin paying back our debts.

This draws us into a paradox, one that comes down to where we really long to see abundance. If we want more for ourselves, then the world will have to become less. But if we discipline our wants and desires, becoming less expansive in our own lives, then the world will be more abundant. And like returning to financial health, this is achieved not merely by cutting back but also by working actively to pay down what we've lost. There is restoration work to be done, damage to be healed. If we redirect all our energies of extraction toward these ends, then human life has an exciting future, full of meaningful work. But it all begins with asking ourselves if we are willing, right now, to change our lives.

Watching the pelicans preen on the sandbar, their feet bright with orange, their bills pink along their bony top and yellow in the membrane of their pouches, I think about that pelican on the sanctuary floor, illustrated in tile. Though the symbol is rooted in an ornithological error, its call toward self-giving love is as solid and true as the ground it stood on. But it is we, not the pelicans, who are called to give of our own lives to revive a dying world. We've killed our own young, in a way, as it is their futures that will be most at risk. But now we should turn to our own life energies and sacrificially offer them for the sake of the renewal of the world. This won't mean pouring out our blood. But it will mean severing our attachments to those realities we've come to see as essential to living the American dream.

There is a passage in Jesus's teaching that sounds like the stuff of a horror film, a break with any meek and mild glow of a Jesus surrounded by a soft light, praying. Teaching a group of his followers, he tells them, "If your hand causes you to stumble, cut it off" (see Mark 9:43).

I learned to understand this passage in a new way several years ago, when I listened to a talk by Ched Myers, a scholar and activist whose understanding of Mark has changed biblical studies. In this talk, Myers didn't start with the Greek of the New Testament, or the social context of the disciples. He began with our society's deep addiction to fossil fuels—an attachment to what we know is wrong and yet cannot let go of. Myers likened our addiction to oil to an alcoholic's attachment to alcohol. Tragically, an alcoholic will drink themself to death, as I've witnessed several times in my life. They know that the alcohol is poisoning them, but they cannot stop. The only solution is a radical severing of the addicted part of themselves—a complete break with the poisoned limb of their addiction.

Many addicts describe the loss of their addiction as a ghost limb. It was so integral to who they were, it was like part of their bodies. And yet, like a gangrenous limb, it was destroying their whole body. The only choice was a radical amputation—not literal but still extremely painful. This, Myers says, is what Jesus is talking about. Through a bold and radical metaphor, Jesus is saying that no moderation or half measures are capable of healing the disordered attachments of our lives. We're beyond bandages and topical antibiotics—we need a complete break with the poisoned part of ourselves.

When I heard Myers, I was reminded of the dark ending to Darren Aronofsky's film *Requiem for a Dream.* It follows a group of characters who are all drawn toward a dream of life and fullness. But each character has an addiction that eventually destroys them. In the final sequence, we find Harry Goldfarb in a dream that repeats an earlier scene in which he runs to embrace his love, Marion Silver. But when he reaches her, she is not there, and he wakes screaming in a hospital bed, his right arm cut off because of an infection in the arm where he shot up heroin. It is a stark, tragic scene, and yet Harry is alive. There's a chance for something else.

This is the best hope we have. It is easy to tempt ourselves, as so many addicts do, into the rationalizations that continue the addiction. But if we are to find any real healing, any hope of even a broken wholeness (and already we have lost so much of the wild world), then we will have to choose to make a strong break with that which diseases us.

The work and sacrifices necessary may seem overwhelming, and yet, as any addict in recovery will tell you, it is better to be free than continue in captivity to a destructive addiction. Life and abundance await. We just have to let our bodies—social, economic, and individual—detox long enough to experience it, cutting off what limbs we must for the healing to come.

The severed arm of our addictions is the negative side of our liberation. But what Christ offered his disciples was more than that. He offered himself to those in desperate need for healing. Christ's work of solidarity was a work of kenosis, a self-offering love, and it is tied to hospitality. Who wants an expansive and dominating host? Instead, we all feel welcomed when someone makes room for us in their lives. It is this making room that we are called to, and it is an act of liberation.

When I go beside the water's edge, as the dusk-tinged clouds set toward their final darkness, and watch the pelicans, with the egrets and ducks and cormorants beside them, I am drawn into a kind of fullness and peace. Standing beside the still waters, I am drawn out of myself, humbled and yet also somehow full, expansive. Here I feel a kind of awe, and I realize that so many of the aims and pursuits of my life—my busy rushing, my worries about success and status—do not really matter at all. Kenosis is an emptying for the sake of fullness. It is a letting go in order to join the wider dance of life. Self-offering, emptying, self-sacrifice—those can sound like scary, annihilating realities. But in the Christian understanding, any limiting of our own desires and wants for the sake of love is a step toward expansion.

Acts of self-restraint for the sake of love have always been essential for human life, but they are even more urgent in our time. Our powers long ago went beyond our wisdom, and still, they increase as we turn over our "intelligence" to machines that lack any sense of depth or wholeness, mirroring only the shallowest aspects of our minds. Such realities are not part of the given world, the kind into which we can settle with a grateful posture, glad to be a part of this common life. The simulations may seem good enough, but they are more demonic for their parasitic proximity to the real. In those places we find a mirror, a dark one, in which our desires are given free play without resistance. In such a world, real love is impossible because real love finds its home in some other person and cannot be contained.

The writer and birder Jonathan Franzen talks about his own journey toward love. Angry at the generalized state of ecological harm, he found himself paralyzed by an abstract hate. He had, in response, stopped caring. "But then, he writes, "a funny thing happened to me. It's a long story, but basically I fell in love with birds." It was from this love for birds, from the exotic to the everyday, that he began to care again about the world. And a curious paradox emerged. "My anger and pain and despair about the planet were only increased by my concern for wild birds," writes Franzen, "and yet, as I began to get involved in bird conservation and learned more about the many threats that birds face, it became easier, not harder, to live with my anger and despair and pain." How did Franzen make such a shift? "I think," he reflects, "for one thing, that my love of birds became a portal to an important, less self-centered part of myself that I'd never even known existed."

This move of love—this decentering of the self beyond the solipsisms of our own approval or disapproval of the world around us—is at the root of kenosis. It is like an idea that the Kabbalist rabbis taught about the creation of the world. The God who is love had, in some strange way, to withdraw to make room for that which is not God. God, the rabbis say, engaged in *tzimtzum*—a limiting of the self, a restraint to make room for the flourishing of creation. These are complex questions, ones philosophers and theologians have been wrestling with for centuries. But the central truth to hold up is this: Love and goodness, by their nature, create room for others.

This pattern of making room is one that spreads in ripples throughout creation. It is no wonder that the idea of the pelican as a self-sacrificing bird came about in the context of a nest. Anyone who has watched nesting birds knows the sacrifice of love that goes into such work. Many birds lose over 20 percent of their body weight while raising young. From incubating eggs to feeding fledglings, they put their energies toward raising their offspring rather than feeding their own bodies. This offering of themselves can be framed in evolutionary terms, of course—the survival of their kind—but that frame would be a dimming down of a larger feature of creation. This dedication, which we feel in our own hearts, is more than mere drives. It is a kind of love, concretely visible in the creation. Even Jesus, when seeking to express his love for the people of Jerusalem, reached for a mother bird as the metaphor for his care: "Jerusalem. . . . How often I have wanted to gather your people just as a hen gathers her chicks under her wings."

In an essay on having children in a time of ecological crisis, the *New York Times* columnist Ross Douthat writes that, "The deepest reason to have more kids . . . is self-centered in a radically different way. It's that if you don't feel cut out for spiritual heroism, if you aren't chaste or poor or particularly obedient, if you aren't ready to be

Mother Teresa—well, then having a bunch of kids is the form of life most likely to force you toward kenosis, self-emptying, the experience of what it means to live entirely for someone other than yourself." To parent well means that we learn to have less. And it is that act of diminishment for the sake of more that the world needs now.

Could birdwatching also be a path toward this kenosis? Echoing Franzen, I think the answer is yes. When our attention is drawn toward creatures totally other than ourselves, creatures who take nothing from us and offer nothing in exchange, we are given the chance to do something selfless, the chance to care beyond any choice bent toward our own fulfillment and survival.

Yes, like anything, including parenting, birding can be a selfish pursuit, typified by Owen Wilson's character, Kenny Bostick, in the film *The Big Year*—a man obsessed by doing whatever is necessary to add another bird to his life list.

But most birders are oriented in a different way. Whatever lists they keep, those lists are only a way into wondering at the incredible variety of birds around them. And I have seen, time and again, birders spring to action when a project or policy threatens the birds they love. Among the strongest conservation organizations I know is the American Bird Conservancy, and its work is echoed by scores of local groups working along similar lines. Just as birds can be icons, windows into a wider world, so caring for their well-being and future can be a way to care for the whole of creation.

I had spent nearly an hour by the water, watching the sandbar. The pelicans had shifted little after resettling once the eagle passed. My sense of obligations at home and work began to tug at me, and I knew it was time to pack up and go. This was during a season when I was trying to see as many birds as possible by bike, a human-powered "big year," of a sort. I had no illusions that I would give up driving to search for birds, but for my health and for the sake of the wild world,

I wanted to find a way to build a habit of birding by bicycle or on foot more than driving.

Askesis is the word the Greeks used for "athletic training," and it's the source of our word *ascetic*. This effort to bicycle to my birding destinations was a form of *askesis*. It was often hard, as I live in a hilly place, and sometimes the weather was bitterly cold or scorchingly hot. Recalling this context—asceticism as training—is important, because being an ascetic isn't simply about dour exercises in self-denial. Proper asceticism has a *purpose*: to train us into different people, to form us so that we can do the hard things necessary for love.

I'm no athlete, but I've done a few triathlons and trail runs. To do those things brings joy, but there is suffering involved to get there. To get the joy out of the suffering, training is required. And so it is with the hard work of love. Love takes training, and care requires the doing of hard things. By engaging in an *askesis* for the sake of birds, we train ourselves for the difficult work of making room. Riding a bike is a small thing, and its impact is minimal, and yet I know that in cycling to see a bird, I am not actively doing damage to the very creatures I love. When I drive, I can't be so sure.

It is no small thing to live, as much as we can, in line with the world as we want it to be. In all those other moments of our lives, when our daily activities are doing damage to the world, we are reminded that we can live into another possibility, that damage isn't inevitable.

As I ride, I follow an old road, long ago closed to cars. A large chunk of the road washed away in a flood a few years back—"the flood of a century" they called it then, though we all know that such measures are now meaningless. Along the road there's a railroad track, which is still active, though not heavily used. The whole stretch can be birdy, full of orioles in the summer and gulls along the water in winter. Up the steep hillsides the forest is preserved by a slope too difficult for construction, so all summer it rings with the songs of Red-eyed Vireos and Indigo Buntings.

Kenosis, in the Christian sense, involves going to the margins. God, in our understanding, became human. But not merely any human: a poor member of a marginal people, a peasant from a backwater ("can anything good come from Nazareth?" Nathanael scoffed when he heard tell that Jesus was the long-awaited Messiah). Birding, too, is an invitation to the margins—a way of finding value in those areas forgotten, hidden, long ago abandoned by most. City dumps, industrial parks, sewer ponds, abandoned golf courses, railroad tracks—these are places birders frequent.

The margins are a place of life, of abundance and activity. *Ecotone* is the word used by ecologists to describe an edge habitat, or a meeting place of two communities of life: grassland and forest, ocean and shore, an urban neighborhood and a mixed riparian woodland, the river against a wooded hillside. When one edge comes up against another, the life of both habitats can thrive. But margins can also be a limiting factor, a fragment into which creatures are pushed. The woodland above me is a remnant, a piece of a much larger wild that once covered this landscape. And the birds that come here are pushed to these margins, just as many people are, making a life in the only place left for them.

From paved-over urban landscapes to farmlands cleared of everything but a cash crop, the varied habitats that birds need often remain only in those places too swampy, too neglected, or even too dangerous to do anything else. Water, in particular, has proven to be a place of margin. For all the aqueducts and retainment ponds, drainage and gutters—water remains a powerful and difficult-to-tame reality, one that will bite back against all but the most careful respect for its power. As the washed-out road attests, for all the efforts of the corps of engineers, water can never be entirely tamed.

In her book, *How to Do Nothing: Resisting the Attention Economy*, artist and birder Jenny Odell shares her rediscovery of the creek that ran through her childhood neighborhood in the San Francisco Bay area of California. Odell had been introduced to the idea of bioregionalism, a way of rethinking geography according to ecological boundaries rather than political or industrial ones. For bioregionalism, where one is from might be better expressed in terms of watershed than in terms of city or state.

After looking at some aerial maps of the neighborhood where she grew up, Odell realized that the Saratoga Creek ran right through it. "In my memory it was just 'the creek'; it didn't come from anywhere in particular nor was it going anywhere," she writes. Then she remembered that there was another creek that ran by the school where she attended kindergarten. That creek too had a name she'd never known until looking at the map: Calabazas Creek. Odell decided to trace the connections the creek formed, looking back to its source and then joining a friend in wandering its channeled path down to the San Francisco Bay.

"Nothing is so simultaneously familiar and alien as that which has been present all along," writes Odell. She walked along the creek, witnessing the buildings that had become the basic geography of Cupertino. And yet this invisible creek had been there for centuries and would remain for centuries more. "Long before cars drove from Whole Foods to the Apple campus, the creek moved water from Table Mountain to the San Francisco Bay. It continues to do this just as it always has, and whether I or any other humans care to notice."

As I biked east, I passed a juncture where I could have turned north. Just a few miles from there was once a water park where I was baptized. Now, as a priest in a church with an ornate marble font, I admit that the idea of getting baptized at a water park with a wave pool and concession stands is a bit strange. Still, that was where I made my profession of Christian faith. Water, for Christians, carries with it all those powerful, life-giving currents that keep the margins protected. But water, as we know, can also bring death. The Christian practice of baptism is one in which we enact a kind of symbolic death. The baptized are buried in the water and raised again to a new life. It's a powerful symbol, and I was honored to have both my daughters baptized as infants. It is a strange thing to acknowledge death when a child has only been alive for a short while. And yet, the ancient wisdom reminds us, if we are unwilling to let go of our life we are not able to really live.

This is the truth at the heart of kenosis. It is the truth of all life, for it is the attempt to escape death that brings death and destruction and a diminished world. It is only when we learn, like those legendary pelicans, to offer our own life for the sake of others, that we can participate in the greater wonder of the world's life.

By the time I reached the final hill toward my house, a winding paved path through a public park, my legs were beginning to burn with the exertion. Still, for all the pain of the effort, my heart remained at the water's edge, watching those giant, strange white wonders. I know I am not able to do all I should, and that I can't do it alone, but I want to live in such a way that these birds keep coming, each fall, to sit on that sandbar. To welcome them again, and have my great grandchildren welcome them too, I know I must learn to live with less. I must offer something of my own comfort and fullness for the sake of the greater abundance of all.

12

DECEMBER

Friendship

WE GATHER IN the dark, David's car pulled off in the muddy gravel by the gate. My eyes are still crusty with sleep, and the coffee I hastily made hasn't yet kicked in. Still, the energy of the day has begun—all of us straining together to listen. I've brought a small Bluetooth speaker, and through it I blast a recording of the deep, growling voice of a Barred Owl—"Who cooks for you? Who cooks for you?" the recording repeats. After a round of playing, we stop and listen. No answer.

I try another voice, an Eastern Screech Owl. Still nothing. In the dim glow of the predawn light, we shrug. Rarely do we succeed in getting an answer. Then, just as we are about to give up, the deep question echoes through the silhouetted trees: "Who cooks for you!" Barred Owl. The first bird of the day.

We are here for the Little Rock Christmas Bird Count, Section 4. Over the day, our small group will count every bird we see or hear—from common House Sparrows to rare surprises like Sandhill Cranes—in this nearly pie-shaped slice of the Little Rock Christmas Bird Count circle. David, our section leader, has birded this same area on the second Saturday of December for over thirty-five years. I joined the group in 2017 at the invitation of Bill, who'd been at it longer than any of us, with over forty years of birding the section. And new this year was Ariana—a birder who brought our average age down by nearly a decade. At this predawn rendezvous it is David, Ari, and me. Bill, now in his eighties, excused himself from any predawn starts. He would join us later, after his daily breakfast at Burger King.

As the light began to show in the east, David asked us to call it: What would be the first bird of the dawn chorus? There's a moment before full daybreak when birds begin to sing their morning songs, welcoming the day and announcing their presence after the night. "White-throated Sparrow," I offered. "Thrasher," David said. "Cardinal," bet Ari. From the thicket of privet in front of us we soon heard an Eastern Towhee—all of us were wrong.

We stood together, counting off the birds we heard as David made tick marks on the list, a clipboard dangling from his neck. "Two chickadees," "Golden-crowned Kinglet," "Ruby-crowned Kinglet," "Hermit Thrush," "Six grackles overhead." We went on, tallying the birds until we had heard every Northern Cardinal, every White-throated Sparrow, every individual bird we could pick from the noisy mix of calls and songs.

It might be easy to assume birding is a solitary pursuit. But the truth is that birding is a place of gathering—the communal seeking of a shared love. The birding world is full of festivals and clubs, field trips and counts. There are message boards and email listservs, WhatsApp Groups and Discord channels, where birders discuss everything from identification to the latest rare bird sightings, from conservation challenges to the best truck-stop food near a birding hotspot. Just as most birds are social creatures, so are the birders who follow them.

Since birding gets at something so basic to human beings, it attracts people from all walks of life, every social class. While so much of our life is siloed into narrow divisions, and birding has historically been a largely white and privileged pursuit, birding still has the ability to bring together people across a wide swath of humanity. And that broadness is only growing with organized efforts for inclusion like Black Birders Week and bird tour companies partnering with Indigenous guides.

Not long ago, I was invited to take part in a day of birding at a farm in South Arkansas, right at the edge of the Mississippi River. It is a place of an amazing convergence of bird species, and so were the birders who gathered to see them. In the parking lot, luxury cars parked beside beat-up sedans with fishing gear in the back, Christian ichthus symbols on bumpers were next to Darwin fish on hatchbacks. There were farmers, professors, stay-at-home mothers, pastors, lawyers, building contractors, carpenters, field biologists, and people of who knows what other occupations, all drawn together through our shared love of birds.

And this is just to name birders: those who have taken up binoculars and the work of identifying species as a serious pursuit. Paying attention to birds is a nearly universal human activity, and though birding as a hobby might be a privileged thing, the love of them need not be. Tell people you know something about birds, and they will come with their stories, their wonderings, their observations of the feathered world that is so closely intertwined with our own. I have met many people I would have never had a conversation with merely because I happened to walk by them with binoculars around my neck.

Age divisions are also bridged in birding, a place where friendships can be forged across decades. Bill, who invited me to this Christmas Bird Count group, had known me since I was twelve. That was the age at which I began my own serious pursuit of birding, and Bill was a well-known fixture of the local Audubon Society. He was in his fifties then, and had himself begun birding as a teenager.

After I'd gone on several birding field trips with the society, my parents let me join obliging adults like Bill on birding outings. Long before I could drive, these adults would pick me up in the early morning to go in search of Henslow's Sparrows in a salt prairie, longspurs at a rural airport, or warblers at a forested state park. Along with a handful of other young birders, I formed friendships with people from twice to seven times my age.

During my college years and just after, birding had become a less central feature of my life. I lost touch with Bill and other friends in the Audubon Society as my interest and circles shifted. But then, after leaving for graduate school and returning, I rekindled my pursuit of birding and, with it, connections with many of those old birding friends. Bill and I renewed our friendship, oddly enough, when the priest at Bill's church had to leave suddenly one Sunday for a family emergency. I was called on to fill in. While delivering my hastily prepared sermon, I looked out at the congregation, and there was Bill, sitting in a pew and smiling up at me. I didn't even know he attended church there. After the service we gladly shook hands and agreed to meet soon. It turned out Bill lived only a few blocks from me, and soon we began to bird together again. When the call for Christmas Bird Count participants came, Bill requested that I be assigned to his group. And that is how I found myself, once again, traipsing into the swampy woods of southwest Little Rock.

There is a path we follow each year after the dawn chorus has quieted. It is an access road, I think, for the sewer mains that run through the woods. Muddy and rutted with ATV tracks, these woods aren't visited too often. There is a creek nearby, Fourche Creek, that is the primary watershed of the city. This means that the water from most of the culverts and storm drains of the streets flows, eventually, to the creek. Because of this, the woods are filled with trash of every kind, from illegally dumped tires to all manner of Styrofoam and plastic. Anything that could float in a flood makes its way down the creek and ends up tangled in the trees. Still, there are trees and shrubs, and with them a haven not only for trash but for wildlife. The walk into the woods not only helps us survey the area fully but usually gets our day started with a decent list of birds.

The itinerary each year is the same: We begin with the trail, walk back through a residential neighborhood, then on to a couple of nearby parks, with a break for lunch in between. In my time with the CBC circle, we've only varied from this path once, when a flood blocked a main road. I didn't set this rhythm of the day, but I've joined it and see its wisdom. From sunup to sundown, we travel through the birdiest parts of our territory, consistently picking up species in their varied niches.

There is a kind of fidelity in this kind of birding—a routine of place and a common pattern of movement. Such fidelity is key to friendship, when you think about it: Friendship is easier when you know where to find someone. On the second Saturday of December, you could likely find our little group somewhere on this same series of stops, rarely more than half an hour off the usual itinerary.

Like deer in the woods or cows in the pasture, we follow the same path, year in and year out. In doing so, our little group becomes a part of the landscape—members of it.

Such fidelity is not unique to my group. When Geoff LeBaron, the chief compiler of the Christmas Bird Count for the National Audubon Society announced his retirement after more than three decades, he looked back on the experience of the CBC. "It's been talked about many times, but one of the primary reasons the Christmas Bird Count has continued to be so successful isn't just a great bird-filled day in one of our favorite locations, it's also about sharing that day with longtime friends and new birders. The social aspects of the CBC are the glue that holds the whole thing together." Though he collects and tabulates the data from thousands of counts from across the country, LeBaron has been participating in the same Christmas Bird Count circle in Rhode Island for over forty years, even when it meant traveling from National Audubon Society headquarters. And I'm sure his story, like ours, is one of many across the country.

Fidelity involves a staying with one another, even as we age and encounter our own mortality. Birders who started in the vigor of their thirties find, after thirty or forty years, that the miles walking are no longer as easy, the cold and wet days of December are harder to stay through. Over the years, Bill began to miss our predawn gathering. He couldn't wake as early, and he couldn't get his own breakfast made. A man of habit, he insisted on waiting until the Burger King down the street opened. Bill began to meet us after our initial hike through the woods, in the parking lot of a defunct public golf course.

This shift was at times frustrating. For all the beauty of routine, Bill became more and more attached to his way of living in the world. He refused to make use of a cell phone, though he technically kept an old flip phone with him for emergencies. If our plans changed, it was hard to reach him. We often had to wait until he finally showed up at the meeting place. Forbearance, often enough, is required for any variety of fidelity, including friendship. Bill had long had a curmudgeonly streak, and that only grew with the decades.

When we met Bill in the parking lot, he moved slowly to pull on his signature rubber boots. It was a kind of Mister Rogers transition Bill would always repeat before going into the field, his loafers giving way to thick wool socks and knee-high British-style "wellies." It was in the lot that Bill first met Ariana, the two of them forming a bridge across the generations: Bill, a staid octogenarian whose loves, outside of birding, included pipe organ music, and Ari, a tattooed, queer birder in their twenties. It was an unlikely pairing, and yet in large part thanks to Ari's enthusiastic friendliness, they hit it off as Ari deftly learned to speak loudly enough for Bill's failing ears.

Bill seemed a bit unsteady as he stood up from the back seat of his car, bracing himself against the door as he stood from pulling on his boots. He steadied himself, and we began our walk around the tree-lined edge of the old golf course. As far as birds go, this was a good spot—a mix of open grasslands with a scattering of tall trees in a kind of artificial savannah edged by denser forest. There were three birds this park consistently delivered—Red-headed Woodpecker, Brown-headed Nuthatch, and Rusty Blackbird.

The last was rarely found by any of the other groups in the count circle, so we felt a kind of responsibility to deliver.

To remain faithful to a particular place over time layers it with stories. Each year new experiences get etched into the terrain, turning trees or fields or ditches into the landmarks of encounters with particular birds. As we walked down the hill, we remembered the time we saw an elusive Wilson's Snipe hiding in the marshy edge of a field, and that time a pair of Purple Finches perched in the snag across the pond. Some of the places hold memories before my own time, and yet the stories have been repeated so many times that the memories *seem* like my own. We always check the same spot along a power-line cut, because a decade ago Bill and David found a Sedge Wren there.

Though this was Ariana's first time with us, the memories would soon become theirs as well. We were all joining in the collective and cumulative experience of a particular relationship with this one place. The land itself was also an old friend, joined in our common fidelity.

December in Arkansas can be hit or miss, varying from sun with relative warmth—often in the fifties—to wet and cold, our hands aching even beneath our gloves. This day was the wet and cold kind, with the clouds beginning their slow drizzle at the time we were farthest away from our cars. Thankfully, there were some old golf-course gazebos still in place, and we shuffled into one to scan the low ground for Rusty Blackbirds.

There was a large flock of blackbirds, made up mostly of Common Grackles and Red-winged Blackbirds, but we scanned through the rolling mix, searching for the brown hues of the appropriately named "rusty" birds. We were pleased to find a handful, off to the side of a group of Common Grackles, glad for another species. Though this was not a competition like a Big Day, there is still an impulse to find as many species as possible, especially one that no other count group would likely have on their list.

As we left the pavilion and continued walking, Bill seemed to begin leaning to his left. It was an odd position, but when we asked him if he needed help, he refused. Bill has long had a stubborn streak and is loath to receive help, a trait that seemed only to worsen as he has needed more of it. Yet as we continued, it was clear there was no way he was going to walk all the way back unassisted.

We settled on getting Bill to wait at the base of the hill while one of us went to the top to drive his car down. It worked, and we got him in the vehicle and to lunch without a fall.

Friendships are built around routines—spots and common places. The television show *Friends* was right to feature Central Perk, a coffee shop where the various members of the circle could meet up. Sometimes the place itself can even be the foundation of the friendship. For birders, a popular local "hotspot" can be a gathering place to initially meet the people known only as a name on eBird, or the local bird discussion list online. I've often pulled up to find another birder scoping a popular place, only to find that I've known the person's interesting bird finds for years without ever having met them in person. Whether it is a wildlife refuge, a coffee shop, or a restaurant—regularity of time and place builds the basis of relationship.

For our Christmas count, our lunch spot, year after year, is Kitchen Express—a soul-food diner where plates are filled cafeteria style and we can be eating a hearty meal in a matter of minutes. It may cost us some birds, this half hour inside. But it's a good chance to catch up with our lists and warm up on a cold count day. Fried catfish accompanied by greens and cornbread can give the body what it needs to get back in the field and keep birding through the wet and cold until sundown.

Sitting down at the table together, rather than just snacking between stops as I usually do on a day of birding, also gives us the chance to turn from looking out and around to looking across the table. I see most of the people on my team only once or twice a year, but it is surprising how our common purpose and our common love of birds can lend itself to a sense of closeness. There is something important about showing up, again and again, that makes friendship possible.

To share a meal is fundamental to friendship. There is something almost primal about the act—a sign of closeness and kinship. If we are sharing a meal together, it is sharing, too, in our space and resources. And that is important, especially for a team working together.

When our meal was complete, Bill wanted dessert—banana pudding crusted with vanilla wafers. The extra food required our patience, but that too is a key part of friendship. The theologian Stanley Hauerwas writes that our friendships with people reflect a larger invitation to friendship with God. The patient presence of friends, he writes, is like prayer: "To learn to pray means our lives must be made vulnerable to God. It requires time and patience to wait on the Lord, and surely the same time and patience are what make friendship possible."

Hauerwas goes on to say that God has overcome our impatience by teaching us to be friends with one another, even our enemies. To be a friend, we must be patient and willing to give, no matter the frustrations. That is a hard lesson to learn, but birding has brought me into a life with people I wouldn't otherwise imagine sharing time. They haven't been enemies, exactly, but they have been people who see the world in starkly different ways than I do. Yet we are joined around a shared attention, and that becomes a point at which our horizons of understanding can find a bridge. It is shared attention, philosopher Charles Taylor has said, that makes language itself possible. Communication is rooted in the same reality as communion, and we are participants in it, whether we gather around a church altar or a Formica-topped table.

After lunch, we headed to Western Hills—another public golf course-turned-park. Bill, always tenacious, wasn't ready to bow out of birding the rest of the day, so he joined us as we began our walk along the cracked and decaying asphalt golf-cart paths.

At the pond near the parking area, a reliable Pied-billed Grebe dipped beneath the water's surface, popping back up with its brown-gray feathers glistening in the afternoon sun, its black-banded bill covering the whole front of its face. Nearby there was a small raft of Ring-necked Ducks. These ducks tend to be found more on ponds and shallower waters than some other diving ducks, and they are among the worst-named species on any list of birds. The ducks have a clearly visible white band around their bills that would make them a good candidate for the name "Ring-*billed* Duck," a title no other duck in the world has. Instead, they are called Ring-necked ducks, based on a trait that is hardly ever visible except in the best light.

We were joined at this park by Ruth and Chuck, two birders who live near the park and bird it regularly. Looking at the ducks, we all shared a groan of dislike for their nonsensical name. It's a complaint that gets repeated year after year, one that of course we can't do anything about. Yet there is something about the repetition of this common frustration that helps with the bonds of friendship. A friendship built on grievance is unlikely to be a good or lasting one, but good friends do often share in a grievance or two, a shared complaint about the world. Mild annoyances, like the poor naming of a species, can be a fixing agent in the glue of friendship.

The post-lunch journey around the park began well enough. There is a pace of birding that is slow and deliberate, a creeping along. You can be attentive to every slight rustle of leaves. Birds are alert to the speed of creatures moving around them. Quickness can be a sign of danger, a hawk crashing down from above, a fox leaping forward from a hiding place. By walking slowly, we are able to notice more ourselves, and birds are less likely to dart from our path. We can always safely assume that the birds have seen us before we see them.

The terrain smoothed into a slightly undulating river bottom. Unsteady from the start, Bill walked down the slight slope from the pond, his rubber boots back on. Still, despite the slow pace of birding, Bill was walking so slowly it was difficult for us to adjust to his pace. Now, several yards from our cars, he was becoming unsteady once again. It soon became clear that this was going to be a shorter loop through the park than normal. We rotated in twos, walking on either side of Bill to make sure he didn't fall, even as he protested that he didn't need help.

By the time we reached the cars, before the light of the day began to wane, Bill was extremely fatigued. When we insisted that he not drive himself home, Bill relented. Since David had picked me up earlier that morning and Bill lived close by, I drove Bill home in his car, followed by David and Ari. We all worked together to get Bill out and up the steps to the door of his apartment building. He wouldn't let us help him in and up the stairs to his second-floor apartment, but he promised to call one of us when he arrived at his bed—a promise he fulfilled a few minutes later.

That was Bill's last Christmas Bird Count, the end of decades in the field. I did go birding with Bill a few times after that day. He had recovered some of his strength, but he was clearly aging in both body and mind.

One day I got a call from him, asking if I would help him drive to the hospital. I drove the short distance to his apartment and helped him get checked into the ER. There he stayed for a few days, dehydrated, suffering a mix of age-related diminishments.

When he moved to his sister's house to recover from that hospital stay, Bill called me to report on the mix of birds that came to his sister's bird feeders. Dan, an ornithologist who had once taken Bill's decades of meticulous bird records and uploaded them to eBird, went to visit Bill and took him birding on a short, paved trail. Bill was part of a church, a community that cared for him, but I think it was his birding friends that visited him most often.

After that stay at his sister's house, he never went home. I helped to move him to assisted living, loading up my trailer with his bed and a few belongings. Bill gave me many of his birding books, field guides to places like Peru and Europe where he had once traveled. In some were the signatures of the authors, people Bill had known and birded with all those years ago.

Just before the final moving day, Bill called and said he wanted to stop by my house. He and his sister arrived, and Bill, moving with a slow, arthritic gait, got out of the car and opened the trunk. Inside was his Swarovski spotting scope, mounted on a sturdy carbon-fiber, Italian-made Manfrotto tripod—an expensive setup that I had used with Bill on our birding outings over the prior years.

It was a major upgrade to the scope I was using at the time, one that I would have been years away from affording on my own budget. Bill and his sister said that they wanted me to have the scope. Bill would no longer be needing it, his years of major birding adventures behind him, his eyesight such that he could no longer use the scope.

A few weeks later, on a late February day, I drove to Two Rivers Park, a peninsula where the Maumelle River pours into the Arkansas River. Over the pedestrian bridge and along a sandy path flanked by horsetails, I went to the inlet where I watch pelicans and gulls, ducks and migrant shorebirds. The usual sandbar was well exposed, playing host to a crowd of gulls, with a few American White Pelicans towering over them in a mixed mass of white. Most were the common Ring-billed Gulls, spanning the various plumages of their ages. I was able to pick out a couple of Herring Gulls, large lumbering birds with yellow bills tipped with a circle of red near the end.

But then, with the new power of Bill's scope, I was able to see a gull that stood out from the others. Its mantle was darker, its legs yellow rather than the pink of the other species there that day. Gulls are hard to identify, and you need to be cautious before putting a bird identification out there that could trigger rare bird alerts. But there is also a community aspect to bird ID, a sharing of expertise and knowledge. I put my phone to the lens, snapping as many pictures as I could, and sent them to a couple of gull identification experts I know. "What do you think of this bird?" I asked. Having friends to text with such questions is part of being in the birding community.

Kenny, another birder I'd known from my teenaged birding days and now one of the best birders in Arkansas, confirmed my suspicion and hope. This was a Lesser Black-backed Gull: a rare species in Arkansas that shows up only a few times each year in the state and hardly ever in my county. I wouldn't have had a chance of identifying it without Bill's scope, and I called him to tell him so.

The passing on of the scope from Bill to me happened years ago now. Still, whenever I look through the crystal clarity of my Swarovski, sorting through a group of sandpipers or examining a far-away loon, I think of Bill, our friendship, and the birding that brought us together. This scope is like a token of friendship I get to carry with me into the field. It's a tool the makes the birding better, just as Bill's company once did.

Sometimes we think that friendship, in its purest form, is spiritual. But I find that the best and most enduring friendships are built on common landscapes and shared love, on the memories of an embodied life together and the tracks we etched walking alongside each other on the trails. I cannot pass the levee outside Holla Bend National Wildlife Refuge without remembering when Bill and I found the state's first Fork-tailed Flycatcher there, or the salt pan prairie where he helped me see my first Henslow's Sparrow. In those memories Bill was not much older than I am now. Through my friendship with him, I know what lies ahead. And I hope that I have friends, both young and old, who can help my journey toward the inevitable day when it will be me, passing along the tools that I can no longer use.

Once more it is the second Saturday in December. The sun has yet to rise, and we stand, the three of us, listening in the dark for the answer of owls. No response. "What will the first bird be?" David asks. We give our replies before hearing a long clear note from a White-throated Sparrow beneath the privet hedge.

Bill won't be joining us this year, as he lives in a nursing home now. But as we walk the familiar route of our Christmas Bird Count day, we repeat the stories that include him. Remember that Sedge Wren you and Bill found here? Remember the Sandhill Cranes that flew over this spot? The landscape holds together a friendship in which I'm a participant, a member, just joining in.

Late in the day, my daughters, ages eight and twelve at the time, joined us as we walked the trails of Western Hills. As we traveled along the cypress swamps of Fourche Creek, an American Woodcock exploded from its hiding place just a few feet away. We were all thrilled at the sighting of this elusive bird, one we had only seen once before in my time on the Christmas Bird Count. With that sighting, this spot would become a new site for our memory, a place we will pass and say, "Remember when . . .?" That memory is now with my daughters. It is now being forged in the next generation who will travel these trails, looking together at the wonder of the birds that share this place.

I went to see Bill a few weeks ago. He was very happy for my visit, though he was uncertain who I was. His memory, which had begun to fade years earlier, had become much worse since his move into assisted living.

"We used to watch birds together," I told him.

"We did?" he answered, with wonder-filled puzzlement.

I showed him the photos of some birds I'd seen recently. He knew all their names, those memories etched deep within him, past the touch of dementia. I didn't feel sad when I left, though I felt for the pain of the loss affecting Bill. That he no longer remembered me was just part of that fading that we will all go through, some day, gradually or all at once. I knew that, no matter Bill's own memory, our friendship still existed. It was still there: in all our years in the field together, in all those moments of shared attention to the wonders of these winged creatures that so caught our eyes.

There is a book by the theologian John Swinton called *Dementia: Living in the Memories of God.* The title gets at its central message. It is God, ultimately, who will remember us when we can no longer remember ourselves. But we get hints of that in human, fleshy form through our companions in life. Our identity comes not through our own making, at least not all of it. Our identity is given and kept through our family and friends, those who watch and wonder alongside us. And when we forget those journeys ourselves, it is they who hold them, telling again the stories we have lost.

In Wendell Berry's novel *Hannah Coulter*, there is a scene in which Hannah, a woman who has lived the whole of her life in the close-knit, fictional farming community of Port William, Kentucky, reflects on the lives of her children. They have been pulled away from what she calls "the membership" that marks the deep belonging of that place. "One of the attractions of moving away," Hannah reflects, ". . . is being disconnected and free, unbothered by membership. It is a life of beginnings without memories, but it is a life too that ends without being remembered." As one of Hannah's friends says to her, "the membership . . . keeps the memories even of horses and mules and milk cows and dogs."

I have lived most of my life in the same place, returning again and again after my various leavings. I have forged long friendships around various shared loves and common values. But it is through birding that I have experienced the fullness of the kind of membership of which Berry writes. It is through birding that my belonging, my membership in this place, has been held. Memories of human companions have etched the landscape with the stories of the other creatures who share this place.

These stories, this common life of wonder, would not be possible without friendship and the faithful presence it cultivates and requires.

AFTERWORD

THIS MORNING, I sat before my icons in silent prayer, a beeswax candle flickering against the wood. I had a timer going, and just before it came to its final bell, I heard a bird outside, a warbler with an unfamiliar voice. I listened and remembered—this was a Mourning Warbler! An elusive bird that migrates each spring through a thin corridor of the country. Should I abandon my prayer and go look? This too is prayer, I heard within.

From my desk drawer, I pulled out my spare binoculars and carefully opened the shed door to look outside. I saw the warbler, yellow with a gray-and-black bib, flitting in an elderberry tree I'd planted in my backyard. I started an eBird list to record the bird, a species that, though not rare, I was unlikely to find again this spring. After spending several minutes with the warbler, recording its song and wondering at its beauty, the bird moved on and I set about the work of the day. That work was finishing this book.

Going through various edits, I got a text from Ari: "You have a Mourning Warbler in your yard???" Ari had seen my report on eBird and was both jealous and congratulatory. I was glad for the affirmation—this was an amazing bird for an urban yard, one that was here because of the habitat I had worked to create. It seemed fitting for such a bird to come as I closed the work on this book. It spoke to hope and hospitality, abundance and friendship.

It is moments like these that keep me grabbing my binoculars and going outside to be amazed. Now is the time to watch and to wonder.

ACKNOWLEDGMENTS

THERE ARE FAR more than twelve spiritual practices I could have been explored in these pages. Among those left out is gratitude. Here, at least, I get a chance to show some gratitude for those who helped bring this book about.

I would have had little to write about without my companions in wonder. There are too many birders to name, but I owe a special thanks to David Luneau, Ariana Remmel, and Evan Garner with whom I shared many of the adventures in this book. Evan, both a fellow birder and priest, was especially helpful in offering comments on several draft chapters of this book.

This book is dedicated to Bill Shepherd and the Arkansas birding community whose members were pivotal in my introduction to birding. Bill's own memory has faded, but the lessons he taught in looking and listening remain with me and many others.

A special thanks is owed to Valerie Weaver-Zercher, my editor at Broadleaf. This book was conceived in conversation with Valerie and brought to a much more readable finish through her many good edits.

Finally, as always, I'm grateful to Emily Sutterfield. Though not a birder herself, she shares my love of the wild world. When life gets heavy, or I get off kilter, it is Emily who always tells me to "go birding!" With Emily, I'm thankful for our two daughters, Lillian and Lucia. I hope that they will experience the abundant joy I've found in the natural world long into the future.

NOTES

Chapter 1: January

2 ***The Catholic priest and writer Henri Nouwen notes:*** Henri J. M. Nouwen, *Behold the Beauty of the Lord: Praying with Icons* (Ave Maria Press, 2007), 24.

5 ***John of Damascus, who lived outside the reach of the Christian emperor:*** William C. Placher, *A History of Christian Theology: An Introduction* (Westminster John Knox, 1983), 93.

5 ***About a century later, another theologian, Theodore of Studios:*** Placher, *A History of Christian Theology*, 94.

13 ***The philosopher Slavoj Žižek calls such moments:*** Slavoj Žižek, *The Fragile Absolute, Or, Why Is the Christian Legacy Worth Fighting For?* (Verso, 2001), 128, emphasis in original.

14 ***As L'Engle recounts, an Antarctic encounter with penguins proved to be such a door:*** Madeleine L'Engle, *Penguins and Golden Calves: Icons and Idols* (Harold Shaw Publishers, 1996), 14.

Chapter 2: February

19 ***as I learned from the theologian William Cavanaugh:*** William Cavanaugh, *Being Consumed: Economics and Christian Desire* (Eerdmans, 2008), 46–47.

21 ***"The world of the icon," he writes:*** John Chryssavgis, "A New Heaven and a New Earth: Orthodox Chrisian Insights from Theology, Spirituality, and the Sacraments," in *Toward an Ecology of Transfiguration: Orthodox Christian Perspectives on Environment, Nature, and Creation*, ed. John Chryssavgis and Bruce V. Foltz (Fordham University Press, 2013), 156.

21 ***"it is a dance of life":*** Chryssavgis, "A New Heaven," 157.

22 ***Permaculturalist Brock Dolman calls watersheds:*** Brock Dolman, "Basins of Relations: A Reverential Rehydration Revolution,"

2008 Bioneers Conference, video posted October 26, 2017, 25 min. 51 sec., https://bioneers.org/brock-dolman-basins-of-relations-a-reverential-rehydration-revolution-bioneers.

23 ***"they hummed of mystery":*** Cormac McCarthy, *The Road* (Vintage, 2006), 286–287.

28 ***"but of synchronizing the actions of men":*** Lewis Mumford, *Technics and Civilization* (Routledge, 1934; 9th imp., 1967), 13–14.

31 ***Karl Marx once wrote:*** Karl Marx, *Grundrisse*, trans. Martin Nicolaus (Penguin, 1973), see https://www.marxists.org/archive/marx/works/1857/grundrisse/ch01.htm.

34 ***"Time is the revealer of love":*** Hans Urs von Balthasar, *The Grain of Wheat: Aphorisms* (Ignatius, 1995), 4.

Chapter 3: March

38 ***"On God's part creation is not an act of self-expansion":*** Simone Weil, *Waiting on God*, trans. Emma Craufurd (HarperCollins, 2001), 89.

39 ***It is as Gerard Manley Hopkins said in his poem of creation:*** Gerard Manley Hopkins, "God's Grandeur," Poetry Foundation, accessed June 25, 2025, https://www.poetryfoundation.org/poems/44395/gods-grandeur.

51 ***"Do anything, however small":*** Gilbert Keith Chesterton, *The Outline of Sanity* (Methuen, 1928), 95.

Chapter 4: April

60 ***"I've become attached to this term 'ruderal,'":*** Lisa Wells, *Believers: Making a Life at the End of the World* (FSG, 2021), 8–9.

62 ***"This is the good life":*** Craig Foster, "How to Find the Wild in a Tame World," interview by Tim Ferris, *The Tim Ferris Show*, no. 735, May 5, 2024, https://tim.blog/2024/05/05/craig-foster-of-my-octopus-teacher-transcript.

64 ***"The priest is the one who freely takes the world in his hands":*** John Zizioulas, "Proprietors or Priests of Creation?," accessed July 10, 2025, https://www.orth-transfiguration.org/proprietors-or-priests-of-creation.

66 ***"Like an amulet worn around the neck":*** L. M. Sacasas, "Amulets Against the Spirit of the Age," *The Convivial Society* 5, no. 12, November 20, 2024, https://theconvivialsociety.substack.com/p/amulets-against-the-spirits-of-the.

67 ***"I suggest that we are thieves in a way":*** M. K. Gandhi, *Trusteeship*, comp. Ravindra Kelkar, ebook, accessed July 10, 2025, https://www.mkgandhi.org/ebks/trusteeship.pdf, 2.

67 ***"The religion and the environmentalism of the highly industrialized countries":*** Wendell Berry, "Word and Flesh," in *The World-Ending Fire: The Essential Wendell Berry*, ed. Paul Kingsnorth (Counterpoint, 2017), 232.

Chapter 5: May

84 ***They focus on the "the promotion of human flourishing":*** The Strother School of Radical Attention, accessed July 10, 2025, https://www.schoolofattention.org/our-story.

85 ***"If we learn to read the birds":*** Jon Young, *What the Robin Knows: How Birds Reveal the Secrets of the Natural World* (Houghton Mifflin Harcourt, 2012), 173.

87 ***"Modernity," writes Rosa:*** Hartmut Rosa, *The Uncontrollability of the World* (Polity, 2020), 28.

90 ***"There was a strange stillness":*** Rachel Carson, *Silent Spring* (Mariner, [1962] 2002), 2.

Chapter 6: June

98 ***"We are just money grubbers":*** "The Death of the Lord God Bird," *Science History Institute*, May 11, 2021, https://www.sciencehistory.org/stories/disappearing-pod/the-death-of-the-lord-god-bird.

98 ***Which bodies are grievable?:*** Hannah Malcolm, "Climate Grief and Christening the World," presented to the Ekklesia Project Gathering, July 2024. A published version of this essay appeared as "The Ethics of Local Belonging: A Theology of Naming Place," *Studies in Christian Ethics* 37, no. 4 (November 2024): 825–843.

98 ***"Precisely because a living being may die":*** Judith Butler, "Precariousness and Grievability," Verso Books (blog post),

November 16, 2015, https://www.versobooks.com/blogs/news/2339-judith-butler-precariousness-and-grievability.

104 ***"To see this many individuals and species dying is a national tragedy":*** Phoebe Weston, "Birds Falling Out of the Sky in Mass Die-Off in South-Western US," *The Guardian*, September 16, 2020, https://www.theguardian.com/environment/2020/sep/16/birds-falling-out-of-the-sky-in-mass-die-off-in-south-western-us-aoe.

106 ***Wendell Berry at another time wrote in one of his poems:*** Wendell Berry, "How to Be a Poet," accessed July 10, 2025, https://www.poetryfoundation.org/poetrymagazine/poems/41087/how-to-be-a-poet.

107 ***as the American Bird Conservancy notes:*** "Northern Bobwhite," ABC's Bird Library, accessed July 10, 2025, https://abcbirds.org/bird/northern-bobwhite.

107 ***"The great obstacle is simply this":*** Berry, "Word and Flesh," 232.

108 ***"Sin is disconnection":*** Elizabeth Oldfield, *Fully Alive: Tending to the Soul in Turbulent Times* (Brazos Press, 2024), 73.

Chapter 7: July

112 ***"Beauty brings copies of itself into being":*** Elaine Scarry, *On Beauty and Being Just* (Princeton University Press, 1999), 3.

116 ***A mere 25 percent:*** Larry Buchanan and Francesca Paris, "'Weird and Daunting': 7,000 Readers Told Us How It Felt to Focus," The Upshot Newsletter, *The New York Times*, August 1, 2024, https://www.nytimes.com/2024/08/01/upshot/experiment-focus-painting-art.html.

118 ***Strassmann calls this "motor birding":*** Joan Strassman, *Slow Birding: The Art and Science of Enjoying the Birds in Your Own Backyard* (TarcherPedigree, 2022), 34–45.

121 ***"Beauty always takes place in the particular":*** Scarry, *On Beauty and Being Just*, 18.

121 ***"An eye for beauty":*** Louis Menand, "What Comes Naturally," *The New Yorker*, November 11, 2002, https://www.newyorker.com/magazine/2002/11/25/what-comes-naturally-2.

123 ***"what I find myself wanting is not just to see beauty":*** Jason M. Baxter, *Why Literature Still Matters* (Cassiodorus Press, 2024), 30.

124 ***Reflecting on these encounters in conversation with Indigenous trackers:*** Craig Foster, *Amphibious Soul: Finding the Wild in a Tame World* (HarperOne, 2024), 157.

Chapter 8: August

130 ***"We're limiting birds to the fallibility of humanity":*** Ariana Remmel, "What's in a Bird Name?," *Audubon Magazine*, Summer 2022, https://www.audubon.org/magazine/summer-2022/whats-bird-name.

131 ***As Pete Dunne writes of the Killdeer's call:*** Pete Dunne and Kevin T. Karlson, *The Shorebirds of North America* (Princeton University Press, 2024), 110.

133 ***"wilderness is where things can be done":*** Marilynne Robinson, "Surrendering Wilderness," *The Wilson Quarterly (1976–)* 22, no. 4 (1998): 60–64, http://www.jstor.org/stable/40260385.

135 ***Recognizing the myriad problems of naming, she writes:*** Malcolm, "Climate Grief and Christening the World."

Chapter 9: September

141 ***"Pelagic birding has a cult quality":*** Peter Dunne, *The Feather Quest: A North American Birder's Year* (Houghton Mifflin, 1999), 237.

142 ***"Works of imagination come of an impulse":*** Wendell Berry, *Imagination in Place: Essays* (Counterpoint, 2010), 3–4.

143 ***As Dunne recounts Debi's instructions:*** Dunne, *The Feather Quest*, 238.

144 ***What we create through language can:*** Charles Taylor, *The Language Animal: The Full Shape of the Human Linguistic Capacity* (Belknap, 2016), 344.

145 ***"perceptual judgments must be laden with theory":*** Paul M. Churchland, *Scientific Realism and the Plasticity of Mind* (Cambridge University Press, 1979), 35.

149 ***"If we are walking on the road":*** "Jizz (Birding)," Wikipedia, last modified July 31, 2024, https://en.wikipedia.org/wiki/Jizz_(birding).

154 ***"Writing is magic":*** David Abrams, "The Ecology of Perception: An Interview with David Abrams," *Emergence Magazine*, July 20, 2020, https://emergencemagazine.org/conversation/the-ecology-of-perception.

Chapter 10: October

163 ***"Silence," wrote R. S. Thomas:*** R. S. Thomas, "The Untamed," *Poetry Foundation*, accessed July 10, 2025, https://www.poetryfoundation.org/poems/52741/the-untamed-56d23175bbdc9.

163 ***"Money-getting men," writes Walton:*** Sir Izaak Walton, *The Compleat Angler, or The Contemplative Man's Recreation* (Modern Library, 1996), 6.

165 ***Among the most famous of those scraps is this:*** Blaise Pascal, *Pensées*, trans. A. J. Krailsheimer (Penguin, 1995), 37.

166 ***"Not knowing how to wait is idolatry":*** Jacques Derrida, *Hospitality*, vol. 1, trans. E. S. Burt, ed. Pascale-Anne Brault and Peggy Kamuf (University of Chicago Press, 2023), 242n41.

166 ***"Speed," as the theologian Stanley Hauerwas has put it:*** Stanley Hauerwas, *The Character of Virtue: Letters to a Godson* (Eerdmans, 2018), 84.

167 ***Raymond Kethledge and Michael Erwin define solitude as a time when:*** Raymond M. Kethledge and Michael S. Erwin, *Lead Yourself First: Inspiring Leadership Through Solitude* (Bloomsbury, 2017), xx.

168 ***"Let him who cannot be alone beware of community":*** Dietrich Bonhoeffer, *Life Together*, trans. John W. Doberstein (Harper & Row), 77–78.

169 ***There is a book by the French Christian mystic:*** Pierre de Causade, *Abandonment to Divine Providence* (Cosimo Classics, 2007), 32.

172 ***"living at nature's pace":*** Gene Logsdon, *Living at Nature's Pace: Farming & The American Dream*, rev. ed. (Chelsea Green, 2000), ix.

Chapter 11: November

177 ***"When the pelican first sees her chicks hatch":*** Hildegard von Bingen, *Hildegard von Bingen's Physica: The Complete English Translation of Her Classic Work on Health and Healing*, trans. Priscilla Throop (Healing Arts Press, 1998), 192.

179 ***Williams was writing of the fate of her beloved Great Salt Lake:*** Terry Tempest Williams, "I Am Haunted by What I Have Seen at Great Salt Lake," *New York Times*, March 25, 2023,

https://www.nytimes.com/2023/03/25/opinion/great-salt-lake-drought-utah-climate-change.html?searchResultPosition=7.

186 ***"my love of birds became a portal":*** Jonathan Franzen, "Liking Is for Cowards: Go for What Hurts," *New York Times*, May 28, 2011, https://www.nytimes.com/2011/05/29/opinion/29franzen.html.

186 ***From incubating eggs to feeding fledglings:*** *Rolf Norberg*, "Temporary Weight Decrease in Breeding Birds May Result in More Fledged Young," *American Naturalist* 118, no. 6 (1981): 838.

187 ***"The deepest reason to have more kids":*** Ross Douthat, "The Case for More Children," *Plough Magazine*, November 18, 2020, https://www.plough.com/en/topics/life/parenting/the-case-for-one-more-child.

190 ***"In my memory it was just 'the creek'":*** Jenny Odell, *How to Do Nothing: Resisting the Attention Economy* (Melville House), 249.

190 ***"Long before cars drove from Whole Foods to the Apple campus":*** Odell, *How to Do Nothing*, 253.

Chapter 12: December

197 ***"It's been talked about many times":*** Geoff LeBarron, "An Age of Transition at the Christmas Bird Count," *Audubon Magazine*, December 7, 2023, https://www.audubon.org/news/age-transition-christmas-bird-count.

201 ***The theologian Stanley Hauerwas writes that:*** Stanley Hauerwas, *The Character of Virtue: Letters to a Godson* (Eerdmans, 2018), 68.

207 ***"One of the attractions of moving away":*** Wendell Berry, *Hannah Coulter: A Novel* (Shoemaker & Hoard, 2004), 133–134.